SANDERS'

UNION SPELLER:

BEING

A CLEAR AND COMPLETE EXHIBITION

OF

ENGLISH ORTHOGRAPHY AND ORTHOËPY,

ON

THE BASIS OF THE NEW ILLUSTRATED EDITION OF WEBSTER'S GREAT AMERICAN DICTIONARY,

TOGETHER WITH

NUMEROUS EXERCISES IN SYNONYMS, IN OPPOSITES, IN ANALYSIS, AND IN FORMAL DEFINITION; THE WHOLE ADAPTED TO THE USE OF SCHOOLS AND ACADEMIES.

BY CHARLES W. SANDERS, A.M.,

AUTHOR OF "SERIES OF SCHOOL READERS;" "ANALYSIS OF ENGLISH WORDS;" "ELEMENTARY AND ELOCUTIONARY CHART," ETC., ETC.

NEW YORK:
IVISON, BLAKEMAN, TAYLOR, & COMPANY,
138 & 140 GRAND STREET.
CHICAGO: 133 & 135 STATE STREET.
1872.

PREFACE.

The aim in this book has been to bring into shape, suitable for daily use in the schools, the clear and complete exhibition of English Orthography and Orthoëpy, found in the last edition of Webster's great American Dictionary.

The plan adopted for this purpose is, in several respects, quite out of the beaten track for works of this kind.

This will especially appear in the series of exercises on the powers and uses of the vowels, which, though prepared for this special purpose, have, nevertheless, all the simplicity of ordinary spelling lessons.

It will appear, also, in the method employed for the illustration of the several Rules for Spelling, which are here supported, not, as is usual, by a few instances, however appropriate, but by such an array of examples, all digested into lessons of convenient size, as can not fail to fix in the mind of the learner the means of determining at once the true spelling of *thousands* of words.

In the collection of Test Words, too, will be found a feature singularly useful for the higher classes in schools, and for Teachers' Institutes; embracing, as it does, over *two thousand* words, so arranged as to reveal many similarities and differences that ordinarily escape the attention of youth entirely.

The whole is eminently *practical*. It shows the laws and usages of the language in respect to *spelling* and *pronunciation*, it explains by *comparison*, by *contrast*, by *analysis*, and by formal *definition*, the true meaning and application of words; yet all this is done without cumbering the path of the pupil with any perplexing details of theoretic teaching.

The treatise on the *Powers and Uses of the Letters*, the list of *Proper Names*, *Foreign Words* and *Phrases*, with their *definitions*, as well as the description of *Pauses* and *Marks* used in *writing*, can not fail to be regarded as essential elements in every well-arranged Spelling Book.

New York, *July*, 1865.

Electrotyped by Smith & McDougal, 82 and 84 Beekman St., N.Y.

SANDERS'

UNION SPELLER.

SECTION I.

ORTHOGRAPHY.

ORTHOGRAPHY treats of letters, syllables and words.

LETTERS are marks, or characters used to represent the sounds of the human voice, heard in speaking. The number of letters in English is twenty-six. In respect to form, they are distinguished as *capitals* and *small letters.* In respect to the sounds they are employed to represent, they are either *vowels* or *consonants.*

A VOWEL represents a free, uninterrupted sound of the voice. The vowels are *a*, *e*, *i*, *o*, *u*, *y*. *W*, also, when preceded by a vowel in the same syllable, has sometimes the force of a vowel, as in the words *few*, *cow*, *power*. *I*, followed by a vowel in the same syllable, as in *alien* (*āl yen*), is a consonant; so, also, is *y*, as in *yet*. *U*, after *q*, and sometimes after *g* and *s*, is a consonant equal to *w*, as in *quit* (*kwit*), *languid*, *assuage*.

A DIPHTHONG is the union of two vowels in the same syllable; as *oi* in *oil*. If, however, *one* only of the vowels is sounded, the diphthong is called *improper*.

A TRIPHTHONG is the union of three vowels in the same syllable; as *ieu* in *lieu.*

A CONSONANT is a letter that represents a sound of the voice, modified by some interruption from the organs of speech. The consonants are separately considered in Section II.*

A SYLLABLE is a letter, or a combination of letters, uttered by one emission of the voice; as, *boy*, *boy'ish.*

A WORD is a syllable, or a combination of syllables, significant of some thought, or idea; as, *house*, *manly.*

A word of *one* syllable is called a MONOSYLLABLE, a word of *two* syllables, a DISSYLLABLE, a word of *three* syllables, a TRISYLLABLE, a word of *four* or more syllables, a POLYSYLLABLE.

A PRIMITIVE WORD is one derived from no other word; as, *fear.*

A DERIVATIVE WORD is one formed from a primitive, by means of prefixes and suffixes; as, *fear less*, *re turn.*

A SIMPLE WORD is one not compounded; as, *milk*, *man.*

A COMPOUND WORD is one composed of two or more simple ones; as, *milkman*, *nevertheless.*

ACCENT is a special stress of the voice, which distinguishes one syllable above others in the same word; as, *hap' py*, *be dew'.*

Accent is either *primary*, as that on the last syllable of *in tend'*, or *secondary*, as that on the first syllable of *su' per in tend'.*

ORTHOEPY treats of the proper *pronunciation* of words, as Orthography treats of their proper *spelling.*

SECTION II.

POWERS AND USES OF THE LETTERS.

VOWELS.

Each of the vowels has its *regular long*, *short*, and its *occasional* sounds which are distinctly marked in the Key, pages 14 and 15. All these various vowel sounds, as also some that are *exceptional*, will be found fully illustrated in the opening exercises of this book.

CONSONANTS.

B.

B has but one sound, as in *bid*, *rib*. Before *t* and after *m* in the same syllable, it is generally silent, as in *debt*, *bomb*. It is, also, silent in *bdellium*.

C.

C has the sound of *s* before *e*, *i*, or *y*, as in *cent*, *cite*, *cyst*, *doc' ile*. This is its soft sound. Before *a*, *o*, *u*, *l*, or *r*, as in *cat*, *cot*, *cut*, *clot*, *crop*—before *k*, *s*, or *t* final, as in *hack*, *optics*, *act*, and, also, when it ends a word, or a syllable not followed by *e*, *i*, or *y*, as in *lac*, *tac tic*, it has the sound of *k*. This is its hard sound. In a few words, it has the sound of *z*, as in *sice* (*size*), *suffice*, *sacrifice*; in some cases, it is silent, as in *Czar*, *indict*, *victuals*, *muscle*.

D.

The regular sound of this letter is heard in *sad*, *date*, *madden*; after a whispered, or sharp consonant in the same syllable, it has the sound of *t*, as in *missed* (*mist*), *vexed*. In *Wednesday*, *handsome*, *handkerchief*, and *wind' row*, it is silent.

F.

This letter has but one sound, as in *flame*, *soft*, *staff*, except in the word *of*, which is pronounced *ov*. It is never silent.

G.

G, before *a*, *o*, and *u*, as in *gale*, *gore*, *gun*, has, except in the word *gaol* (*jāle*), a hard sound; also, before *l* and *r*, as in *glad*, *grope*, and *occasionally* before *e*, *i* and *y*, as in *get*, *give*, *logy*. It has this hard sound always at the *end* of a word, or a syllable not followed by *e*, *i*, or *y*, as in *beg*, *big*, *bog*; so, too, when doubled, as in *begging*, *biggest*, *boggy*. Before *e*, *i*, and *y*, however, with very few exceptions, *g* has its soft sound, as in *gem*, *ginger*, *gypsum*, *rigid*. In a few words, *g* has the sound of *zh*, as in *rouge* (*roozh*). Before *m* and *n* it is silent, as in *phlegm*, *sign*, *gnat*.

H.

H represents a mere breathing, or aspirate, as in *home*, *hat*. It is silent after *g*, as in *ghost*, after *r*, as in *rhyme*, as also when preceded by a vowel in the same syllable, as in *oh*, *Jehovah*.

J.

J has very nearly the sound of *dzh*, being the precise equivalent of *g* soft, as in *jibe*. In *hallelujah*, (when spelled with *j*,) it has the sound of *y*. It is never silent.

K.

K has but one sound, as in *ken*, *kin*. It is silent before *n* in the same syllable, as in *knight*; also after *c*, as in *back*.

L.

L has but one sound, as in *lame*, *land*, *miller*. It is sometimes silent, especially before a final consonant, as in *calm*, *walk*, *would*, *half*.

M.

M has but one sound, as in *make*, *clam*, *hammer*. It is silent before *n* in the same syllable, as in *mnemonics*.

N.

N has two sounds,—that heard in *note*, *ten*, *nail*, and that in *linger*, *link*, *uncle*, which latter is *essentially* the same sound as that represented by *ng*. This sound it has, as a general rule, before *g*, *k*, *c*, *q*, and *x*, as in *anger* (*ang' ger*), *link*, *cinque* (*sink*), *zinc*, *minx*.

P.

P has but one sound,—that heard in *pen*, *lip*, *hop*, except in the words *cupboard* (*kŭb' urd*) and *clapboard* (*klab' bōrd*), where it has the sound of *b*. It is silent, when initial, before *n*, *s* and *t*, as in *pneumatic*, *psalm*, *ptarmigan;* so, also, in a few other cases, as in *receipt*, *corps* (*cōre*), *raspberry*.

Q.

This letter always occurs before *u*, and the two (*qu*) together have the sound generally of *kw*, as in *quiet* (*kwīet*). In some words, however, *qu* has the sound of *k* only, as in *coquette* (*cokĕt'*), *antique*.

R.

Before a vowel in the same syllable, as in *ream*, *dream*, as also when *between* two vowels, the first of which is short, as in *băron*, *mĕrit*, *flŏrid*, the letter *r* has a rough, or trilled sound. In other situations, it has a smooth or palatal sound, as in *far*, *form*, *terse;* while in others still, it has this smooth, or palatal sound combined with an obscure vowel sound, somewhat like that of *u* in *urge*, as in the words *fare*, *ore*, *our*. *R* is never silent.

S.

This letter has two sounds; one sharp and hissing, as in *sin*, *mist*, the other flat and buzzing, as in *has* (*haz*), *amuse*.

S, with its sharp sound, following a liquid or another *s*, and coming before a letter with the sound of *y* consonant, (as *i* in *version*, *mansion*, *passion*,) also, in some cases, where it comes before *ū*, (as in *sūre*, *sugar*), has the sound of *sh*. In some words *s* alone has this sound, as in *nausea* (*naushea*), *Asiatic*.

S, preceded by a vowel in an accented syllable, and *followed* by a vowel with the sound of *y* consonant, in connection with the latter vowel, generally has the sound of *zh*; thus, *vision* (*vizhun*), *fusion* (*fuzhun*), &c.; so, also, in *scission*, *abscission*, *rescission*. *S* is silent in a few words, as in *aisle*, *isle*, *island*, *demesne*, *puisne*, *viscount*, and mostly at the end of French words, adopted in English, as, *chamois* (*sham' my*).

T.

The proper sound of *t* is heard in the words, *take*, *note*, *latter*. When *t precedes ia*, *ie*, and *io*, and, at the same time, *follows* an accented syllable not ending in *s* or *x*, it has the sound of *sh*, as in *patient* (*pa shent*), *station*, *partial*, &c. Preceded by *x* or *s*, the *t* and *i* preserve each its own separate sound, or together assume the sound of *ch*, as in *mixtion* (*mikst' yun*, *or mik' chun*), *question*, &c.

V.

The true sound of this letter is heard in *vale*, *civil*, *live*. It is never silent, except in *sevennight* (*sennit*).

W.

W, *before* a vowel in the same syllable, is a *consonant*, with a sound closely resembling *oo* in *moon*, as in the words *wet* (*oo et*), *wine*, *twine*, *reward*; *after* a vowel, however, in the same syllable, it is either altogether *silent*, as in the words, *grow*, *grown*, or, with the vowel preceding, forms a diphthong; thus, *few* (*fū*), *new* (*nū*), *cow* (*ow* like *ou* in *our*), *power*. Before *r*, in the same syllable, *w* is silent, as in *wring* (*ring*), *wrote*, as also in the words *answer* (*anser*), *toward* (*to' ard*), and *two* (*too*).

X.

X has two sounds—that of *ks*, as in *tax* (*taks*), which is called its sharp sound, and that of *gz*, as in *exist* (*egzist*), which is called its soft, or flat sound. When commencing a word, it has the sound of *z*, as in *xebec* (*zebec*).

Y.

Y, when a *consonant*, always precedes a vowel in the same syllable, as in *you*, *halyard*. When a *vowel*, it has exactly the same sound as *i*; thus, *hymn* (*him*), *tyrant*.

Z.

The regular sound of *z* is heard in *zone*, *maze*, *hazy*. In some words, it has the sound of *zh*, as *seizure* (*seez yur*). In *rendezvous* (*rĕn' de vōō*) it is silent.

CH.

CH has nearly the sound of *tsh*, as in *child*, *much*, *richly*. In some words, it has the sound of *sh*, as *chaise*, *machine*. In some, it sounds like *k*, as *chorus*. In *drachm* (*dram*), *schism* (*sizm*), and *yacht* (*yot*), *ch* is silent.

GH.

GH, beginning a word, has the sound of *g* hard, as in *ghost* (*gōst*). In *hiccough* (*hik' kup*), it has the sound of *p*. In other cases, it sounds like *f*, as, in *draught* (*draft*), or like *k*, as, in *hough* (*hŏk*). After *i*, it is silent, as in *sigh* (*sī*), and generally before *t*, as in *taught* (*tawt*); so, also, in *though* (*thō*), and *through* (*thrōō*).

PH.

PH has usually the sound of *f*, as in *sylph* (*sylf*), *phantom*. In *Stephen* (*steven*), it sounds like *v*. Before *th* initial, it is silent, as in *phthisic* (*tĭz' ik*), as also in a few other cases.

SH.

The proper sound of this combination is heard in *shop*, *shine*, *flesh*. *Sh* is never silent, but the sound which it indicates, is represented variously; by *c*, for example, as in *o ce an' ic*,—by *s*, as in *nausea*,—by *t*, as in *negotiate*,—by *ce*, as in *ocean*,—by *ci*, as in *social*,—by *si*, as in *tension*,—by *ti*, as in *captious*,—by *xi*, as in *noxious*,—by *ch*, as in *machine*,—by *sci*, as in *conscience*, &c.

TH.

TH has a sharp, or whispered sound, as in *thing*, *breath*, *author*, and a flat or vocal sound, as in *thine*, *then*, *mother*. *Th* in *thyme* (*time*), *phthisic* (*tiz ik*), *Thomas* (*tŏm as*), *Thames* (*temz*), sounds like *t*.

WH.

The letters in this combination are sounded as if written *hw*, as in *what* (*hwat*). In *who*, *whole*, and *whoop*, the *w* is silent.

ZH.

The *sound* represented by this combination, is heard in the words *fusion*, (*fuzhun*), *brasier* (*brazhér*), and some others, though the combination itself never occurs in the proper spelling of any English word.

ASSIMILATION OF CONSONANTS.

The consonants called flat, vocal or sonant, and those called sharp, aspirate or surd, have a marked correspondence to each other. Thus, each *flat*, in the list following, has, immediately under it, its corresponding *sharp*:—

b, *v*, *th* (as in *thine*), *d*, *z*, *zh*, *g*, *flats*.
p, *f*, *th* (as in *thin*), *t*, *s*, *sh*, *k*, *sharps*.

In the attempt to pronounce a *flat* and a *sharp*, in one and the same syllable, either one of the letters will become silent, or be assimilated to the other. Thus, in the words, *debt* and *subtle*, *b* being a *flat* and *t* a *sharp*, the *b* is not heard at all; for we pronounce these words as if written *det*, *sŭt' l*.

In forming the English Possessive Case, on the other hand, as *lad's*, for example, we often bring together two consonants that are pronounced with ease, if pronounced at all, only by assimilating the *sound* of the one to that of the other; so that while to the *eye*, as in the above example, we have *lad's*, to the *ear*, the word is *lad'z*, that is, *s* which is *sharp* has, in reality, been changed into *z*, which is *flat*, so as to correspond with the *d*, which is, also, flat.

This affinity between the two classes of consonants is, also, seen in forming plurals by the addition of *s*, as *dogs* (*dogz*), in the third person singular of verbs, as *boards* (*boardz*), and in affixing *ed* to form certain Preterits and Participles, as, *marked* (*markt*), *missed* (*mist*). See note, page 45.

KEY TO THE PRONUNCIATION

VOWELS.

REGULAR LONG AND SHORT SOUNDS.

ā, *long*, as in...............āle, fāte, rāy.
ă, *short*, as in...............ădd, făt, hăve.
ē, *long*, as in...............ēve, mēte, pēace.
ĕ, *short*, as in...............ĕnd, mĕt, lĕopard.
ī, *long*, as in...............īce, pīne, mīre.
ĭ, *short*, as in...............ĭll, pĭn, admĭt.
ō, *long*, as in...............ōld, nōte, lōaf.
ŏ, *short*, as in...............ŏdd, nŏt, tŏrrid.
ū, *long*, as in...............ūse, tūbe, feūd.
ŭ, *short*, as in...............ŭs, tŭb, bŭt.
ȳ, *long*, as in...............flȳ, stȳle, relȳ.
y̆, *short*, as in............... cy̆st, ny̆mph, ly̆ric.

OCCASIONAL SOUNDS.

â, as in....................âir, câre, beâr.
ä, *Italian*, as in.............ärm, fär, fäther.
ȧ, as in....................ȧsk, grȧss, dȧnce.
a̤, *broad*, as in..............a̤ll, ta̤lk, ha̤ul.
ạ, like short *o*, as in.........whạt, wạnder, wạllow.
ê, like â, as in..............êre, thêre, hêir.
e̱, like long *a*, as in.........e̱ight, pre̱y, obe̱y.
ẽ, as in....................ẽrmine, vẽrge, prefẽr.
ï, like long *e*, as in..........pïque, machïne, polïce.
ĩ, like ẽ, as in..............ĩrksome, vĩrgin, thĩrsty.
ȯ, like short *u*, as in.........ȯther, dȯne, sȯn.
o̤, like long *oo*, as in.........pro̤ve, do̤, to̤mb.
ọ, like short *oo*, as in........bọsom, wọlf, wọman.
ô, like broad *a*, as in........ôrder, fôrm, stôrk.
o͞o, as in...................mo͞on, fo͞od, bo͞oty.
o͝o, as in...................wo͝ol, fo͝ot, go͝od.
ṳ, preceded by *r*, as in.......rṳde, rṳmor, rṳral.
ụ, like short *oo*, as in........pụt, pụsh, pụll.
û, as in ....ûrge, bûrn, concûr.

KEY TO THE PRONUNCIATION.

REGULAR DIPHTHONGAL SOUNDS.

oi, or oy (unmarked), as in...oil, join, oyster, toy.
ou, or ow (unmarked), as in..out, hound, owl, vowel.

CONSONANTS.

ç, *soft*, like *s sharp*, as in.....çede, çite, merçy.
ȼ, *hard*, like *k*, as in.........ȼall, ȼonȼur, suȼcess.
ch (unmarked), as in........child, much, touching.
çh, *soft*, like *sh*, as in........çhaise, maçhine.
ȼh, *hard*, like *k*, as in........ȼhord, ȼhorus, epoȼh.
ḡ, *hard*, as in...............ḡet, beḡin, foḡḡy.
ġ, *soft*, like *j*, as in..........ġem, ġin, eleġy.
s, *sharp* (unmarked), as in....same, yes, rest.
ș, *soft*, or *vocal*, like *z*, as in...hașs, prișm, amușe.
th, *sharp* (unmarked), as in...thin, breath, healthy.
th̶, *flat*, or *vocal*, as in.......th̶ine, smooth̶, with̶er.
ng (unmarked), as in........ring, sing, single.
n̲, as in....................lin̲ger, lin̲k, un̲cle.
x̲, like *gz*, as in.............ex̲ist, ex̲ample, ex̲haust.
ph, like *f*, as in.............phantom, sylph.
qu, like *kw*, as in ....queen, conquest.
wh, like *hw*, as in...........what, when, awhile.

When one letter of an improper diphthong, or of a triphthong, is *marked*, it is to be taken as representing the sound of the combination, and the letter or letters which *are not marked*, are to be regarded as silent, as in āim, clēan, cēil, pēople, grọup, sōul, joûrnal, tōw, &c.

In the following work, all letters printed in *Italics*, are silent. This, however, is done only where mistakes in pronunciation are otherwise likely to be made.

When several words, in the same column, are accented on the same syllable, the *first* only bears the accentual *mark;* so, also, when two or more words, in succession, have each one or more silent letters, occurring relatively on the same syllable, the *first* only is *Italicised*. This rule is, also, observed in respect to all the marks used in this book, to indicate the various sounds of the vowels and consonants.

THE ALPHABET.

ROMAN LETTERS.		ITALIC LETTERS.		OLD ENGLISH.	
a	A	*a*	*A*	𝖆	𝕬
b	B	*b*	*B*	𝖇	𝕭
c	C	*c*	*C*	𝖈	𝕮
d	D	*d*	*D*	𝖉	𝕯
e	E	*e*	*E*	𝖊	𝕰
f	F	*f*	*F*	𝖋	𝕱
g	G	*g*	*G*	𝖌	𝕲
h	H	*h*	*H*	𝖍	𝕳
i	I	*i*	*I*	𝖎	𝕴
j	J	*j*	*J*	𝖏	𝕵
k	K	*k*	*K*	𝖐	𝕶
l	L	*l*	*L*	𝖑	𝕷
m	M	*m*	*M*	𝖒	𝕸
n	N	*n*	*N*	𝖓	𝕹
o	O	*o*	*O*	𝖔	𝕺
p	P	*p*	*P*	𝖕	𝕻
q	Q	*q*	*Q*	𝖖	𝕼
r	R	*r*	*R*	𝖗	𝕽
s	S	*s*	*S*	𝖘	𝕾
t	T	*t*	*T*	𝖙	𝕿
u	U	*u*	*U*	𝖚	𝖀
v	V	*v*	*V*	𝖛	𝖁
w	W	*w*	*W*	𝖜	𝖂
x	X	*x*	*X*	𝖝	𝖃
y	Y	*y*	*Y*	𝖞	𝖄
z	Z	*z*	*Z*	𝖟	𝖅
&		*&*		&	

SPENCERIAN SCRIPT.

a b c d e f g h

i j k l m n o p

q r s t u v w x

y z

A B C D E F G

H I J K L M

N O P Q R S

T U V W X Y

Z

SECTION III.

REGULAR SOUNDS OF THE VOWELS.

LONG SOUNDS.

EXERCISE 1.

ā	ē	ī
āle	mē	īce
ate	we	tie
ace	he	vie
ape	be	hie

EXERCISE 2.

ō	ū	ȳ
nō	ūse	bȳ
go	due	my
so	hue	sly
ho	cue	try

SHORT SOUNDS.

EXERCISE 3.

ă	ĕ	ĭ
ăm	hĕn	ĭf
an	men	it
at	net	is
ax	hem	in

EXERCISE 4.

ŏ	ŭ	y̆
ŏf	ŭs	hy̆p
on	up	lyn
ox	sup	gyp
not	nut	pyx

EXERCISE 5.

ă	ĕ	ĭ	ŏ	ŭ
căb	wĕb	bĭb	cŏb	cŭb
dab	neb	fib	fob	dub
nab	wed	nib	hob	rub
tab	led	rib	job	tub
gab	fed	jib	mob	hub

EXERCISE 6.

Is it an ax? No; the ax is by me.
Is it not an ox? It is an ox.
Is he to do it as we do?
No; he is not to do it as we do.
As we go in, he is to go up.
Is the hen in the tub? She is.
Let the dog run at the fox.
Do not go in the hot sun.
Can we go on the ice, or not?

EXERCISE 7.

ă	ĕ	ĭ	ŏ	ŭ
găd	rĕd	dĭd	sŏb	cŭd
had	ted	hid	lob	mud
lad	zed	kid	nob	rud
mad	ped	fid	bob	fud

EXERCISE 8.

săg	bĕg	bĭg	nŏd	bŭg
bag	keg	fig	pod	rug
rag	leg	jig	rod	hug
fag	peg	pig	hod	dug
lag	teg	wig	sod	tug

EXERCISE 9.

hăm	gĕt	hĭm	bŏg	mŭg
jam	jet	rim	log	jug
dam	yet	nim	dog	sug
man	let	dim	hog	pug
ram	ket	lin	fog	lug

EXERCISE 10.

căn	mĕt	kĭn	cŏn	gŭm
ran	wet	win	don	hum
tan	set	sin	non	mum
van	bet	din	yon	rum
ban	pet	pin	ton	sum

EXERCISE 11.

ă	ĕ	ĭ	ŏ	ŭ
căp	pĕn	sĭp	tŏp	dŭn
map	ten	dip	lop	gun
sap	den	hip	mop	fun
tap	fen	lip	pop	pun
lap	wen	nip	fop	run

EXERCISE 12.

băt	gĕm	pĭp	lŏt	nŭn
fat	yes	tip	jot	cup
mat	sex	rip	cot	pup
sat	kex	bit	sot	hut
vat	vex	fit	box	tut

EXERCISE 13.

săd	kĕn	tĭn	dŏt	bŭn
pan	ben	sip	hot	tun
pap	ret	pit	rot	sun
hat	wex	wit	fox	fud
bad	bed	bid	rob	bud

EXERCISE 14.

The cat ran at the rat.
A fat pig is in the pen.
My pet kid is in the lot.
The lad had a peg top.
The man sat in the log hut.

LONG SOUNDS.

EXERCISE 15.

ā	ē	ī	ō	ū
māte	mēte	mīte	mōte	mūte
made	mere	mice	mode	mule
lace	here	lice	hole	huge
haze	lere	hide	lore	lure
save	sere	side	sole	lute

EXERCISE 16.

ā	ā	ā	ā	ā
bāke	fāce	sāge	hāke	bāte
cade	pace	wage	lake	gate
fade	race	gage	make	date
jade	page	safe	take	pate
lade	rage	fake	rake	hate
wade	cage	cake	sake	late

EXERCISE 17.

ā	ā	ā	ā	ā
hāle	vāle	tāme	sāme	sāne
male	wale	game	bane	vane
pale	came	hame	cane	vase
sale	dame	lame	lane	case
tale	fame	name	mane	base

EXERCISE 18.

ā	ā	ā	ī	ī
cāpe	rāte	dāze	bīte	dīce
nape	cave	gaze	rite	nice
rape	gave	maze	kite	vice
tape	lave	raze	gibe	rice
sate	nave	haze	pice	bice
dale	dade	dace	site	rife

EXERCISE 19.

ī	ī	ī	ī	ī
bīde	līfe	hīve	bīle	vīle
ride	wife	dike	file	wile
tide	dive	like	mile	lime
wide	five	pike	pile	mime
fife	rive	tike	tile	time

EXERCISE 20.

ī	ī	ī	ī	ī
fīne	nīne	pīpe	hīre	rīse
kine	pine	ripe	mire	wise
line	sine	wipe	sire	size
mine	tine	dire	tire	dime
vine	wine	fire	wire	hide

EXERCISE 21.

ō	ō	ō	ō	ō
lōbe	rōde	yōke	mōle	bōne
robe	doge	bole	pole	hone
code	coke	cole	dome	cone
bode	joke	dole	home	lone
node	poke	jole	tome	tone

EXERCISE 22.

ō	ō	ū	ū	ū
cōpe	mōre	cūbe	Jūne	mūse
hope	bore	tube	tune	fuse
mope	core	puke	dune	dupe
pope	pore	duke	cure	cute
rope	gore	fume	mure	pule

EXERCISE 23.

ȳ	ȳ	ȳ	ȳ	ȳ
thȳ	spȳ	prȳ	pȳre	stȳle
sky	shy	cry	lyre	type
fly	dry	sty	chyle	byre
ply	fry	fyke	chyme	syke

WORDS OF TWO SYLLABLES.

LONG SOUNDS.

EXERCISE 24.

ā	ē	ī	ō	ū
bā' by*	rē' al	bī' as	bō' nus	dū' ty
fa vor	fe cal	bi ped	bo ny	fu ry
la bel	he ro	ci der	co lon	hu man
la bor	le gal	di et	co ma	hu mor
la dy	me ter	di al	co ny	lu nar

EXERCISE 25.

lā' ma	pē' on	fī' ber	cō' pal	lū' rid
la zy	re bus	fi nal	do tal	mu cus
ma zy	ve nal	i dol	fo ḡy	mu ral
na ked	ve to	i tem	ho ly	pu nic
na vy	e ra	i vy	lo cal	pu pil

EXERCISE 26.

pā' gan	pē' nal	lī' bel	mō' dal	pū' ny
pa per	ze ro	ti ny	mo lar	su ral
ra cy	te por	ti dy	no mad	tu nic
sa vor	be ṣom	vi per	o dor	u nit
ta per	re gal	vi tal	on ly	tu mid

EXERCISE 27.

vā' por	rē' nal	vī' rus	ō' ral	sū' et
va ry	he lot	mi ṣer	o ver	tu tor
wa ver	he mal	ri ot	o val	tu mor
pa pal	pe rĭ	pi ca	po lar	bu bo
na ṣal	pe wit	mi ca	so da	ju ror

* Note here, as elsewhere throughout the book, that when two or more consecutive words, in the same column, are accented on the same syllable, the *first* only bears the accentual *mark*.

EXERCISE 28.

ā	ē	ī	ō	ū
nā' tal	sē' poy	pī' lot	ō' men	lū' çid
ma jor	ve nus	di do	do nor	mu cid
ca per	ce dar	mi ter	bo lus	mu şic
ca ter	be ing	ri val	to per	cu bic
ha lo	de mon	mi nus	ho mer	du cal

EXERCISE 29.

ȳ	ȳ	ȳ	ȳ	ȳ
hȳ' son	tȳ' ro	dȳ' nam	ġȳ' rāte	hȳ' dra
hy men	ty ler	dy er	ty rant	hy brid
ġy ron	hy po	dry ad	cy as	hy phen
typ al	by ard	ġy ral	wy vern	ly rāte

WORDS OF TWO SYLLABLES.

SHORT SOUNDS.

EXERCISE 30.

ă	ĕ	ĭ	ŏ	ŭ
băl' lot	ĕb' on	bĭd' der	bŏd' kin	bŭf' fet
ban dit	ed dy	big ot	bod y	but ler
ban dy	ed it	bil let	bon net	but ter
ban ner	en ter	bit ter	bon ny	bux om
ban ter	en vy	fit ter	bot tom	bus kin
hat ter	el der	fit ly	cor rel	mus ket

EXERCISE 31.

căb' in	fĕn' nel	dĭn' ner	cŏb' web	cŭl' ly
cam let	fer ret	dip per	cof fer	cum ber
can dor	fer ry	dit to	cof fin	cut ler
can dy	fet id	dit ty	cot ter	cut ter
can ter	fet ter	diz zy	col lar	cut let
bat ter	ep ic	wit ty	bob bin	bud let
lat ter	fel on	cit y	rob in	sut ler

EXERCISE 32.

ă	ĕ	ĭ	ŏ	ŭ
căn′ ton	lĕt′ ter	fĭl′ let	cŏm′ et	fŭn′ ny
car ol	lev el	fil ly	com ma	fuz zy
car ry	lev et	fil ter	com mon	fus tic
cas tor	lev y	fin ny	con fab	gun ny
cav il	ken nel	fit ly	cop y	gun nel

EXERCISE 33.

dăl′ ly	ĕr′ ror	lĭm′ it	dŏt′ ted	gŭt′ ter
dap per	ev er	lim ner	doc tor	lum ber
gaf fer	mer ry	lim pid	fol ly	mus ter
gal lop	jel ly	lin net	fos sil	mut ter
gam mon	jen ny	viv id	fos ter	num ber

EXERCISE 34.

hăb′ it	pĕs′ ter	pĭt′ y	gŏb′ let	pŭb′ lic
hap py	pet ty	pil fer	gob lin	pud der
lad der	ren net	riv et	gos pel	pup pet
mad ly	len til	sim mer	gos sip	pup py
mad am	sel dom	sim per	job ber	rub ber

EXERCISE 35.

măg′ ic	sĕx′ ton	sĭn′ ner	mŏr′ al	rŭd′ der
mad der	set ter	sin ter	mor ris	rud dy
mag net	ted der	tin ner	nog gin	rug ged
pan ic	tem per	sir up	ton sil	rum my
par ry	ten nis	tim ber	hor rid	rum pus

EXERCISE 36.

răb′ id	tĕn′ der	tĭm′ id	hŏb′ by	rŭn′ let
rag ged	ven om	tin der	hop per	rus set
ral ly	ver y	tin sel	hor ror	put ty
rap per	ves tal	tip pet	of fer	suc cor
sad ly	vex er	piv ot	ot to	run ner

EXERCISE 37.

ă	ĕ	ĭ	ŏ	ŭ
lăs′ so	wĕl′ kin	tĭt′ ter	pŏn′ der	sŭf′ fer
sal ad	wel ter	vic ar	con dor	sun ny
sap py	bev y	vic tim	pot ter	sul ly
tab by	pen ny	vic tor	sog ġy	sup per
tab let	reb el	viġ il	sol id	tur ret

EXERCISE 38.

tăf′fy	wĕd′ ded	vĭg′ or	pŏp′ lin	ŭl′ cer
tal ly	vel lum	vis̱ it	tor rid	un der
tal on	ten on	vis̱ or	tot ter	up per
tam per	ten or	vis ta	vom it	ut ter
tat ter	ten et	viv id	yon der	vul gar

EXERCISE 39.

tăr′ ry	tĕn′ don	wĭn′ ner	ŏn′ set	jŭn′ to
tas sel	hec tor	liv er	mot to	lus ty
val et	rec tor	vil la	lob by	tun ny
val id	men tal	sil ly	jol ly	sum mit
vas sal	hec tic	tip sy	tod dy	mun dil

EXERCISE 40.

pat′ ter	ves′ sel	riv′ er	rob′ ber	gun′ ner
ras cal	vel vet	rip rap	pos set	muf fin
vap id	tet ter	lim bo	pop lar	mus lin
rap id	nec tar	nip per	pop pet	pun to
ran cid	res̱ in	rig or	son net	mum my

EXERCISE 41.

y̆	y̆	y̆	y̆	y̆
çy̆m′ bal	hy̆m′ nic	ty̆p′ ic	sy̆n′ tax	hy̆s′ sop
cyn ic	mys tic	tym pan	sys tem	pyx is
cym ling	tym bal	lyr ic	syn od	myx on
cys tic	syl van	pyg my	ġyp sy	gyp sum

SECTION IV.

REGULAR SOUNDS OF THE VOWELS.

LONG SOUNDS.

Two or more vowels combined, of which *one* only is heard.

EXERCISE 42.

āi as ā	āid	pāid	fāith
	aim	pain	main
	fail	rail	paint
	jail	waif	saint
	nail	wait	gain

EXERCISE 43.

āi as ā	brāin	grāin	stāin
	chain	slain	strain
	drain	snail	trail
	flail	sprain	train
	frail	staid	braid

EXERCISE 44.

āy as ā	bāy	jāy	brāy
	day	lay	clay
	fay	may	dray
	gay	nay	fray
	hay	pay	gray

SUGGESTION.

Here be particular to point out to the pupil that, in each combination, *one* vowel only is *marked*, and *that* only is *heard;* the whole group or combination representing the single sound denoted by the vowel marked; thus, *āi*, in *āid*, is to be pronounced precisely as if the *i* were not there at all; so *ēa* in *bēam* (*bēme*), *ōa*, *bōat* (*bōte*). Let it be well understood that nothing is *heard* but the *regular long sounds* of the several vowels, (*ā*, *ē*, *ō*, &c.), though another vowel, in each case, appears to the *eye*.

EXERCISE 45.

āy as ā	rāy	eā as ā	breāk
	say		greāt
	stay		steak
	sway	āo as ā	ġāol (*jāle*)
	tray	āu as ā	ḡāuġe
	pray	āye as ā	āye (ā)

EXERCISE 46.

ēa as ē	bēad	dēan	hēap	mēal
	beak	each	heat	mean
	beam	ear	lea	wean
	bean	eat	leaf	near
	deal	fear	lean	neat

EXERCISE 47.

ēa as ē	pēa	sēat	fēast	blēach
	peak	veal	beast	bleat
	reap	year	least	cheap
	rear	zeal	beard	cheat
	seal	yeast	bleak	clean

EXERCISE 48.

ēa as ē	clēar	lēash	scrēam	snēak
	dream	peach	sheaf	speak
	drear	preach	shear	squeak
	freak	reach	fleam	spear
	gleam	cream	smear	weave

EXERCISE 49.

ēa as ē	tēa	strēam	tēa̤se	blēar
	plea	wheat	cease	heat
	squeal	ream	crease	feat
	steam	yean	lease	treat
	streak	ea̤se	ḡear	meat

EXERCISE 50.

ee as ē	fee	seed	peep	reek
	see	seek	weep	heed
	wee	seem	keep	jeer
	lee	meek	reef	keel
	bee	meet	reel	feel

EXERCISE 51.

ee as ē	keen	feel	three	bleed
	leer	beef	free	breed
	deem	deed	tree	cheek
	deep	veer	glee	cheer
	feed	weed	flee	fleece

EXERCISE 52.

ee as ē	fleet	sheet	speed	steer
	greed	sleek	spleen	street
	green	sneer	squeeze	sweet
	greet	sneeze	steed	sweep
	sheep	speech	steep	teeth

EXERCISE 53.

ee as ē	eel	creed	queer	leech
	wheel	creep	screen	beech
	sleet	sheen	screech	beet
	breeze	sleep	wheeze	beer
	cheese	queen	leek	meed

EXERCISE 54.

ēi as ē	cēil	sēized	con cēive′	de ceit′
	ceil′ ing	seiz′ in	de ceive	re ceipt
	seize	lei sure	re ceive	ei′ ther
	seiz ure	seine	per ceive	nei ther
	weird	sein er	con ceit	seign ior

EXERCISE 55.

iē as ē	briēf	fiēnd	niēce	siēge
	chief	fierce	piece	shriek
	grief	pierce	priest	yield
	thief	tierce	shield	be lief′
	field	tier	wield	re lief

EXERCISE 56.

iē as ē	biēr	liēf	æ as ē	Cæ' ṣar
	pier	riev' er		pæ an
	mien	field ing	œ as ē	Phœ bus
	lien	bre viēr'	ēo as ē	pēo ple
	liege	ar riere	ēy as ē	kēy

EXERCISE 57.

aī as ī	aiṡle (*īle*)	īe as ī	pīe
eī as ī	height		be lie'
	sleight		un tie
	ei' der	oī as ī	choir (*kwīre*)
īe as ī	die	uī as ī	guide
	tie		guile
	lie		guiṣe

EXERCISE 58.

ōa as o	bōat	gōal	rōan	cōax
	coat	foam	goad	hoax
	goat	roam	road	load
	moat	loan	toad	loaf
	coal	moan	woad	soak

EXERCISE 59.

ōa as ō	cōarse	clōak	hōard	ōak
	hoarse	coach	throat	oaf
	board	coast	shoal	oats
	boast	float	roast	oar
	toast	groan	roar	oath

EXERCISE 60.

ōe as ō	fōe	tōe	ōo as ō	dōor
	hoe	sloe		floor
	woe	throe		brooch
	roe	tĭp' tōe	eō as ō	yeō' man
	doe	al oe		yeo man ry

EXERCISE 61.

	gōurd	cōurse	cōurt	shōul′ der
	mourn	four	court′ ly	boul der
ōu as ō	source	pour	court ling	poult
	soul	poured	court ship	poult ry
	soul′ less	pour′ ing	court ing	poul tĭçe

EXERCISE 62.

	dūe	är′ gūe	rĕs′ cūe	en sūe′
	cue	văl ue	fes cue	pur sue
ūe as ū	hue	ven ue	ā gue	sub due
	sue	vĭrt ue	rĕs′ i due	in due
	glue	ven due′	ret i nue	im bue

EXERCISE 63.

	slūice	sūit		neū′ ter
	slui′ cy	suit′ ed		neu tral
ūi as ū	juice	suit or	eū as ū	feud
	jui cy	suit ress		feud al
	nui sance	pur suit′		deuçe

EXERCISE 64.

	dew	clew	newt	re new′
	few	flew	new′ ly	es chew
ew as ū	mew	mewl	a new′	ew′ er
	pew	slew	a skew	skew er
	new	spew	be dew	stew ard

EXERCISE 65.

	pew′ ter	cûr′ few		lieū (*lū*)
	jew el	sin ew	ieū as ū	a dieu′
ew as ū	Jew ish	cur lew		pûr′ lieu
	dew y	mil dew	eaū as ū	beaū ty
	dew lap	Jew ry	iew as ū	view

EXERCISE 66.

	eȳe		eȳ′ er
	eye′ lash	eȳ as ȳ	ey ing
	eye ball		ey as
eȳe as ȳ	eye less		ḡey ser
	eye let	ȳe as ȳ	rȳe
	eye ful	uȳ as ȳ	buȳ

SECTION V.

REGULAR SOUNDS OF THE VOWELS.

SHORT SOUNDS.

Two or more vowels combined, of which *one* only is heard.

EXERCISE 67.

ăi as ă	plăid plaid′ ed plaid ing răil ler y (*răl′ ler y*)	uă as ă	guăr an tee′ guar an teed guar′ an ty guar an tor guar an tĭed

EXERCISE 68.

ĕa as ĕ	dĕad	brĕad	dĕath	rĕalm
	deaf	breadth	dread	spread
	head	breast	dreamt	stead
	lead	breath	health	stealth
	read	dealt	meant	wealth

EXERCISE 69.

ĕa as ĕ	swĕat	brĕak′ fast	jĕal′ ous	stĕad′ y
	threat	stead fast	zeal ous	read y
	thread	peaș ant	mead ow	heav y
	tread	feath er	pleaș ant	dead ly
	zeal′ ot	leath er	head y	lead ed

EXERCISE 70.

ĕo as ĕ	lĕop′ ard jeop ard feoff (*fef*) feof fee′ feoff′ ment feoff er	uĕ as ĕ	guĕss guest
		iĕ as ĕ	friĕnd
		ĕi as ĕ	heif′ er
		œ as ĕ	œs trum
		æ as ĕ	æs thĕt′ ic

EXERCISE 71.

uĭ as ĭ	guĭlt	buĭld	uĭ as ĭ	bĭs cuĭt
	guilt y	built		cĭr cuit
	guilt less	build′ er		guin ĕa
	guild	build ing		cuish (*kwĭs*)
	guills	g̅uĭ tär′	ĭe as ĭ	sĭeve

EXERCISE 72.

ŏu as ŏ	hŏugh (*hok*)	oŭ as ŭ	yoŭng	coŭp′ let
	hough ed		touch	doub let
	hough ing		touch y	coun try
	lough		cous̱ in	flour ish
ŏw as ŏ	*k*nowl edge		cour age	nour ish

SECTION VI.

OCCASIONAL SOUNDS OF THE VOWELS.

EXERCISE 73.

â	ä	ȧ	a̤	ạ
as in *âir*	as in *ärm*	as in *ȧsk*	as in *a̤ll*	as in *whạt*
câre	cär	cȧst	fa̤ll	wạd
bear	ah	gasp	halt	wash
pare	barb	waft	talk	swap
fair	taunt	bask	wa̤rm	wand
lair	guard	past	haul	squat
hair	harm	pant	warn	swab
prâyer	garb	task	warp	squash

EXERCISE 74.

pâr′ ent	bär′ ter	bȧs′ket	wa̤′ ter	wạl′ let
bare ly	car cass	pas tor	hal ter	wan der
char y	bar bet	vast ness	waltz er	wam pum
fair y	bar ley	last ly	daub er	war rant
pair ing	gar ter	mas tiff	false ly	wal rus
dar ing	har ness	cast ing	gaud y	wad ding
care ful	harp er	raf ter	sau cer	wash er

EXERCISE 75.

ê	e̱	ẽ
like â in *âir.*	like ā in *āle.*	like û in *ûrge.*
thêre	prey (*prā*)	mẽrge
their	eight	serve
*h*eir	feint	terse
*h*eir′ ing	skein	hearse
*h*eir ess	o bey′	mer′ cy
*h*eir less	me lee (*mā lā′*)	ear nest

EXERCISE 76.

ĭ	ï	ĩ
as in *pïque* (*peek*).	as in *pïque.*	as in *irk.*
po lïce′	ro̤u tïne′	thĩrst
ca price	çhe nïlle (*shē neel*)	kir tle
va lise	cas sïne	cir cus
ma rine	e̱ lite (*ā leet*)	vir gin
ma çhine	vi ṣite	sir loin
pe lïsse (*pe lees′*)	ra vine	girl ish

EXERCISE 77.

ȯ	o̤	o̥	ô
like ŭ in *sŭn.*	like ōō in *tōō.*	like ŏŏ in *wŏŏl.*	like a̤ in *a̤ll.*
wȯn	do̤	wo̥lf	fôrk
done	move	wolf′ ish	nor′ mal
dove	prove	wolf ish ly	cor ner
love	so̤up	wo̥uld (*wood*)	horn y
come	lo̤ṣe	co̥u*l*d	thorn y
shove	tom*b*	sho̥u*l*d	form al

EXERCISE 78.

cȯv′ er	lo̤ṣ′ er	wo̥m′ an	bôught (*bawt*)
col or	los ing	wom an ly	fought
com pass	do ing	wom an ish	sought
oth er	yo̤uth ful	bo′ ṣom	ought
gov ern	gro̤up ing	bo som ing	brought

EXERCISE 79.

o͞o as in *mo͞on.*		o͝o as in *wo͝ol.*	
bo͞on	fo͞od	bo͝ok	bro͝ok
boot	spoon	hook	soot
cool	gloom	cook	foot
fool	groove	hood	look
doom	swoon	good	crook

EXERCISE 80.

sa lo͞on′	mo͞or′ ing	be to͝ok′	ho͝od′ wink
co coon	hoop ōe	un hook	coop er
pa troon	koo doo	for sook	crook ed
si moon	boor ish	foot′ less	hook ed
doŭb loon	noon ing	book ish	wood y
här poon	mā roon′	look ing	soot y

EXERCISE 81.

ṳ as in *rṳde,* like o͞o in *mo͞on.*		ụ as in *bụll,* like o͝o in *wo͝ol.*	
rṳle	prṳde	pụt	pụl′ pit
frṳit	prṳne	pụsh	bụl ly
rṳs̱e	prṳ′ dent	bụsh	bụl let
trṳe	rṳ mor	pụll	bụsh el
trṳce	rṳ ral	pụl′ ley	bụl wark

EXERCISE 82.

trṳf′ fle	frṳ′ gal	bụl′ rush	bụll′ ock
crṳ el	frṳit y	fụll er	bụl tōw
crṳde ly	grṳ el	fụll ness	pụl let
crṳis̱ er	drṳ id	fụll age	pụll er
crṳ ral	crṳ et	bụl bụl	pụl len

EXERCISE 83.

û as in *ûrge,* like ẽ in *vẽrge.*		y̆ like ẽ in *vẽrge,* or ĩ in *sĩr.*	
bûrn	cûr dle	myrrh (mẽr)	hyrse
furl	curd y	myr′ tle	thyrse
curb	curb ing	syr tic	thyr′ sus
cur′ ry	burgh er	syr ma	thyr soid
hur dle	burg lar	pyr gom	syr tis

EXCEPTIONAL SOUNDS OF THE VOWELS.*

EXERCISE 84.

ee as â	e'er (*âir*) ne'er	ai as ĕ	said (*sĕd*) saith a gain' (*a gĕn*) a gainst
e as ä	ser' geant (*sär-*)		
uay as ē	quay (*ke*)		
a as ĕ	Thames (*tĕmz*)	ay as ĕ	says (*sez*)

EXERCISE 85.

u as ĕ	bur' y (*bĕr ry*) bur y ing bur ied bu ri al bu ri er	a as ĕ	a' ny (*en' y*) ma ny
		e as ĭ	En glish (*ĭng glish*) pret ty (*prĭt ty*)
		o as ĭ	wom en (*wĭm en*)

EXERCISE 86.

u as ĭ	bus' y (*bĭz zy*) bus y ing bus ied bus i ly bus *i* ness (*biz ness*)	ee as ĭ	been (*bin*) breech' es (*brich ez*) breech ing three pence (*thrĭp ens*) steel yard (*stĭl yard*)

EXERCISE 87.

eau as ō	beau (*bō*) flam' beau bū reau plä teau' tab leau	au as ō	haut' boy (*hō boy*) vaude ville (*vōd' vĭl*)
		ew as ō	sew (*sō*)
		eo as ū	feod (*fūde*) feod' al

* By Exceptional sounds are here meant, as will be observed, those not included in the classes already treated of, and illustrated, as *Regular* and *Occasional.* Here is the proper place to bring up in review all the various vowel sounds,—*Regular, Occasional,* and *Exceptional,* and to make the distinctions indicated by these terms perfectly familiar.

SECTION VII.

DIPHTHONGAL SOUNDS.

EXERCISE 88.

oi as in *oil.*

boil	soil	join	void	quoit
coil	roil	coin	coif	quoin
moil	broil	loin	choice	noise
toil	spoil	foin	voice	poise
foil	coix	groin	doit	point

EXERCISE 89.

joint	toil′ et	toil′ ing	a void′	sub′ soil
moist	boil er	loi ter	de void	trē foil
joist	join er	toil some	pûr loin	tûr moil
hoist	nois y	oint ment	em broil	pär boil
foist	joint ly	a noint′	a droit	re coil′

EXERCISE 90.

oy as *oi* in *oil.*

boy	poy	coy′ ly	en joy′	de coy′
coy	cloy	joy ful	an noy	sa voy
toy	troy	boy ish	al loy	en′ voy
hoy	loy′ al	toy ing	de ploy	tom boy
joy	roy al	oys ter	de stroy	con voy

EXERCISE 91.

ou as in *out.*

bout	loud	mound	spout	rout
lout	proud	pound	trout	gout
pout	shroud	round	stout	mount
shout	bound	sound	sprout	fount
snout	hound	found	scout	noun

EXERCISE 92.

pouch	bounce	ac count′	a rouse′	out′ fit
couch	frounce	dis count	es pouse	out let
pounce	flounce	de nounce	ca rouse	boun ty
trounce	wound	an nounce	hous′ ing	coun ty
ounce	ground	pro nounce	mous ing	coun ter

EXERCISE 93.

ow as *ou* in *out.*

owl	brow	brown	howl	drow′ sy
cow	prow	frown	prowl	drows ing
how	scow	crown	cowl	cow er
now	scowl	drown	town	cow ish
vow	growl	clown	down	cow slip

EXERCISE 94.

cow′ ard	pow′ der	bow′ er	cow′ ry	al low′
dow el	vow el	dow er	dow ry	a vow
dow dy	row el	flow er	tow er	en dow
row dy	tow el	fowl er	pow er	re nown
chow der	trow el	show er	pow wow	a down

SECTION VIII.

SILENT VOWELS.

EXERCISE 95.

e final silent.*

mō′ bile	făç′ ĭle	ăġ′ ĭle	pĕn′ sĭle
dĕb ile	grac ile	frag ile	ten sile
flăb ile	doc ile	prō file	scis sile
sôr bile	flex ile	fē brile	mis sile
nū bile	sẽrv ile	vī rile	sub tile

* The letter *e*, when final, is always *silent*, except in monosyllables containing no other vowel (as *he, we, me*), some classical words (as *sim′ i le*), and some words from modern foreign languages. In a monosyllable, however, and in a syllable under the accent, though silent itself, its effect generally is to lengthen a preceding vowel; as *măd*, *māde*; *nŏt*, *nōte*.

EXERCISE 96.

tăc′ tīle	rĕp′ tīle	sĕx′ tīle	mĕn′ ace
fic tile	fēr tile	text ile	sûr face
duc tile	tôrt ile	e dīle	sŏl ace
tract ile	hŏs tile	com pile′	pal ace
fis sile	fū tile	re vile	grĭ mace

EXERCISE 97.

tĕr′ race	ŏf′ fice	cŏp′ pīce	lăt′ tīce
pòm ace	chal ice	com plice	am ice
pĭn nace	mal ice	jäun dice	crev ice
fûr nace	pum ice	sol stice	nov ice
bŏd ice	côr nice	jus tice	sērv ice

EXERCISE 98.

rīd′ dance	sĕm′ blance	dūr′ ance	sī′ lence
guīd ance	pen ance	pĭt tance	es sence
băl ance	cum brance	cā dence	sen tence
val ance	hin drance	cre dence	sē quence
clēar ance	frā grance	sci ence	prŏv ince

EXERCISE 99.

rō mance′	frē′ quence	brō cade′	block ade′
fī nance	cŏm merce	är cade	sca lade
ad vance	ses tērce	căs cade	po made
a mērce	dĭ vōrce′	brĭ gade	gre nade
dis perse	re sōurce	cock ade	pa rade

EXERCISE 100.

cru sāde′	fu see′	măn′ age	re gāle′
de grade	a gree	um brage	em pale
in vade	set tee	fū mage	ga zĕtte
cŏm′ rade	de cree	ròm age	co quette
fī nīte	de gree	nŏn age	brṳ nette

EXERCISE 101.

cā′ ble	cŏb′ ble	quĭb′ ble	foi′ ble
ga ble	gob ble	crib ble	răm ble
ta ble	hob ble	frib ble	bram ble
fa ble	bub ble	treb le	scram ble
sta ble	stub ble	fee ble	trem ble

EXERCISE 102.

thĭm′ ble	jŭm ble	tŭm′ ble	doŭb′ le
nim ble	mum ble	stum ble	troub le
wim ble	rum ble	nō ble	trēa cle
fum ble	crum ble	mär ble	tăck le
hum ble	grum ble	bau ble	mus cle

EXERCISE 103.

a′ ble	făd′ dle	mĕd′ dle	rĭd′ dle
bēa dle	pad dle	ped dle	nod dle
lā dle	strad dle	fid dle	cud dle
cra dle	sad dle	mid dle	scud dle
ăd dle	swad dle	grid dle	fud dle

EXERCISE 104.

hŭd′ dle	twee′ dle	dăn′ dle	dwĭn′ dle
mud dle	ī dle	han dle	cod dle
pud dle	bri dle	kin dle	bun dle
nee dle	si dle	spin dle	trun dle
whee dle	căn dle	brin dle	hûr dle

EXERCISE 105.

nōō′ dle	whĭf′ fle	rŭf′ fle	pûr′ fle
poo dle	scuf fle	waf fle	ēa gle
băf fle	shuf fle	rī fle	bea gle
raf fle	muf fle	tri fle	găg gle
snaf fle	snuf fle	sti fle	drag gle

EXERCISE 106.

ō′ gle	spĕck′ le	sĭck′ le	bŭck′ le
gär gle	freck le	trick le	chuck le
bū gle	fick le	tick le	muck le
căck le	mick le	stick le	suck le
hack le	prick le	cock le	truck le

EXERCISE 107.

spärk′ le	tĕm′ ple	măn′ tle	ca jōle′
trĭp le	stā ple	gen tle	pa role
am ple	stee ple	hûr tle	con sole
tram ple	bee tle	tur tle	pis tole
sam ple	tī tle	băt tle	tad′ pole

EXERCISE 108.

dĭm′ ple	wĭm′ ple	tŏp′ ple	pûr′ ple
pim ple	rum ple	tip ple	dū ple
rim ple	ap ple	nip ple	coŭp le
crim ple	grap ple	crip ple	stärt le
sim ple	rip ple	stop ple	scrṳ ple

EXERCISE 109.

wăg′ gle	trī′ būne	căt′ tle	kĕt′ tle
strag gle	je june′	rat tle	set tle
gog gle	at tune	prat tle	whit tle
jug gle	e lōpe	tat tle	lit tle
strug gle	es cape	wa̤t tle	spit tle

EXERCISE 110.

brĭt′ tle	shŭt′ tle	pŭz′ zle	ex trēme′
bot tle	friz zle	nuz zle	su preme
throt tle	daz zle	rap ĭne	sub līme
cut tle	driz zle	fam ine	ca nine
scut tle	muz zle	jas̤ mine	se rene

EXERCISE 111.

fixt′ ūre	stăt′ ūte	fûr′ tĭve	stăt′ ūre
nûr ture	con clave	pĕn sive	pȧst ure
fil trate	nā tĭve	pas sive	fēat ure
pros trate	vo tive	cos tive	creat ure
frus trate	fĕs tive	rest ive	cŭlt ure
con trīte	post ure	vest ūre	vult ure

EXERCISE 112.

vŏl′ ūme	cär′ mine	chi cāne′	vŭl′ pīne
noi some	prĭs tine	pro fane	tort ūre
mĕm brane	fē line	hu mane	tre phīne′
mun dane	fe rine	cär′ bīne	dĭ vine
ēr mine	lū pine	răpt ūre	sā line
vĕnt ure	joint ure	doc trine	re fine

EXERCISE 113.

ob scēne′	ĕm′ pīre	frĭg′ āte	cē′ rāte
sin cere	um pire	pal ate	pi rate
ạu stere	sat ire	stel late	ĭn grate
re vere	man date	strī ate	ser rate
se vere	leg ate	cli mate	sen ate

EXERCISE 114.

se dāte′	tĕn′ ūre	trēa′ tĭse	be fōre′
ma nure	fig ure	môr tise	de plore
de mure	vērd ure	ăn ise	im plore
ma ture	coif fure	fran chīṣe	ig nore
im mure	nāt ure	pûr chase	se cure

EXERCISE 115.

ue silent after *g* and *q*.

vāg*ue*	lēag*ue*	fa tĭg*ue*′	an tĭq*ue*′
plague	teague	sa rigue	prat ique
vogue	pïque	in trigue	ob lique
rogue	bȧsque	u nique	cri tique
brogue	mŏsque	pro rōgue	o pāque
tȯngue	casque	ha răngue	bûr lĕsque
fūgue	cinque	mo resque	gro tesque

EXERCISE 116.

Words ending in *en* with the *e* silent.

dĕad′ *e*n	săd′ d*e*n	rĭd′ d*e*n	bōld′ *e*n
lead en	red den	trod den	gold en
glad den	bid den	sod den	bound en
mad den	hid den	hoi den	wŏŏd en
broạd en	slid den	wīd en	gär den

EXERCISE 117.

härd′ *e*n	beech′ *e*n	strĕngth′ *e*n	tāk′ *e*n
wạrd en	bĭrch en	ēarth en	blăck en
bûr den	frĕsh en	wēak en	slack en
dĕaf en	length en	shāk en	strick en
stĭff en	hēa then	ōak en	thick en

EXERCISE 118.

sĭck′ *en*	spōk′ *en*	heärk′ *en*	rīp′ *en*
quick en	bro ken	stōl en	shap en
silk en	to ken	swoll en	o pen
drunk en	wo ven	chēap en	hĕmp en
shrunk en	clo ven	flăx en	hap pen
līk en	därk en	mix en	wax en

EXERCISE 119.

shärp′ *en*	whēat′ *en*	frōz′ *en*	tīght′ *en*
chōş en	thrĕat en	sweet en	whit en
lōōs en	ōat en	strāi*gh*t en	molt en
lĕs sen	ŏft en	līght en	lĕnt en
bēat en	soft en	bright en	shôrt en

EXERCISE 120.

ēat′ *en*	bĭt′ ten	rŏt′ ten	crā′ ven
fąll en	kit ten	hĕav en	e ven
băt ten	smit ten	leav en	sĕv en
fat ten	*w*rit ten	hā ven	riv en
flat ten	got ten	ra ven	driv en
vix en	box en	bra zen	miz zen

EXERCISE 121.

Words ending in *en*, in which the *e* is sounded.

ăsp′ en	lăt′ ten	păt′ ten	sī′ ren	flā′ men
chick en	lī chen	plat en	băr′ ren	o men
kitch en	mär ten	row en	ash en	hy men
wąr ren	mȳn chen	wĭck en	pol len	līn en
hȳ phen	pat en	yew en	sul len	breth ren

EXERCISE 122.

Words ending in *on* with the *o* silent.

bā′ con	rĕck′ *o*n	poi′ şon	pär′ son	bŭt′ ton
bēa con	rēa şon	foi son	pĕr son	glut ton
dea con	sea son	prĭs on	lĕs son	mut ton
fą*l* con	trea son	dam son	sē ton	pär don
bĕck on	mā son	crim son	cŏt ton	ar son

EXERCISE 123.

Words ending in *ed*, with the *e* silent.*

bärb*ed*	bēak*ed*	fām*ed*	vẹin*ed*	pāin*ed*
ôrbed	ha̤wked	fumed	gowned	stained
fōrced	skĭlled	ärmed	pȧssed	fẹigned
ho͞ofed	willed	āimed	stärved	strēaked
ärched	missed	grained	vĕxed	wĭnked
harped	wished	rained	boxed	dragged
carped	jumped	drained	hōaxed	bagged
marked	cracked	raiṣed	coaxed	stabbed
stalled	rocked	trained	poached	blabbed

EXERCISE 124.

Words ending in *ed*, in which the *e* is heard.†

ā′ ġed	cûrs′ ed	jăg′ ged	răg′ ged	*w*rĕtch′ ed
blĕss ed	crŭtch ed	leg ged	rug ged	pick ed
crab bed	cusp ed	lĕarn ed	stub bed	fôrk ed
crag ged	dog ged	nā ked	wick ed	brṳiṣ ed
cro͝ok ed	ho͝ok ed	pēak ed	wing ed	be lȯv′ ed

EXERCISE 125.

Words ending in *el* with the *e* silent or very obscure.

bär′ bel	ēa′ ṣel	nā′ vel	shĕk′ *el*	swĭv′ *el*
bē tel	grŏv el	o̤u ṣel	shȯv el	tēa ṣel
chăt tel	hā zel	răv el	shrĭv el	wea ṣel
draz el	măn tel	riv el	sniv el	trăm mel
driv el	mus sel	scȯv el	swin̲ ḡel	pȯm mel

* The e, in *ed*, is silent only when not preceded by *d* or *t*; for if *d* or *t*, (letters of the *same* organ,) precede, the sounding of the final *d*, without an intervening vowel, would be simply impossible. When, however, any other consonant precedes, the *e* is dropped in pronunciation, and the *d* easily combines with it, subject only to the law of assimilation, explained on page 13.

† Those words in which the *ed*, though not preceded by *d* or *t*, forms a separate syllable, are always employed as adjectives; as, *wing′ ed fowls*, *pick′ ed stakes*; when used as *verbs*, the *e* is not heard.

SECTION IX.

CONSONANTS.

EXERCISE 126.

b silent, after *m* or before *t* in the same syllable.*

jăm*b*	tọm*b*	clīm*b*	nŭm*b*′ ness	dĕ*b*t
lamb	womb	plŭmb	dumb ly	debt′ or
limb	dŭmb	crumb	plumb er	doubt
cōmb	numb	clīmb*e*d	cōmb ing	re doubt′
bómb	thumb	lĭmb less	thŭmb kin	doubt′ less

EXERCISE 127.

c like *s*, before *e*, *i*, or *y*.

rāçe	çīte	fĕnçe	çȳme	çy̆st
rac′ ing	cĭn′ der	fan′ cy	cy′ clops	cyg′ net
ra cy	civ il	vis cid	cy press	cyn ic
sa̤uce	cē dar	ac id	cy cle	cyc lic
sau′ cy	ci der	dē cent	cy cas	cyg nus

EXERCISE 128.

c like *k*, before *a*, *o*, *u*, *l*, and *r*.

eāme	eōst	eūte	elīme	erămp
ca′ ter	cō′ cōa	cu′ pid	clŏt	crāy′ on
mi ca	co pal	cŭs tom	clip′ per	crē ole
cär nage	co lon	cum ber	clat ter	crĭs pin
crĕs cent	co hort	cud gel	clas sic	crump et

EXERCISE 129.

c like *k*, before *k*, *s*, or *t* ending a syllable.

jăck′ et	pĭck′ et	bŭck′ et	crăck′ er	lŏck′ er
pack et	rick ets	lock et	pack er	wick er
rack et	tick et	rock et	lack er	back er
plack et	wick et	pock et	bick er	ad dĭct′
brack et	in sect	sock et	pict ure	e lect
rel ics	rel ict	con vict	lect ure	re strict
phyṣ ics	vẽr dict	ē dict	fract ure	af fect

* These brief headings are designed merely to draw attention to what has been more largely stated concerning the several consonants, in Sec. II.

EXERCISE 130.

ce and *ci* like *sh.*	*sc* and *sci* like *sh.*	*sch* like *sh.*	*c* like *sh.*
ō′ cean	cŏn′ scious	schĭst	ō ce ăn′ i ca
an cient	con scious ly	schist′ ic	tes tā′ ce a
so cial	con science	schist ous	crus ta ce a
spa cious	con sci ĕn′ tious	schôrl	e ma ci ate
spe cie	prē′ sci ence	schorl′ y	as so ci ate
spe cious	pre sci ent	schorl ous	e nŭn ci ate
lŭs cious	pre scious	schorl ite	ex crṳ ci ate

EXERCISE 131.

ch like *tsh.*

chāfe	chāpe	chăp′ let	trĕnch′ er	ôr′ chard
chăf′ fer	cham′ ber	chal lenge	clinch er	ûr chin
chal ice	chăp man	chit chat	tēach er	sā chem
chap ter	chär ter	chī na	preach er	săch el
cham fer	chart ism	blēach er	pōach er	fetch ing

EXERCISE 132.

mŭch	brȧnch′ y	en crōach′	in trĕnch′	chĭntz
such	bŭnch y	re proach	re trench	chat′ ty
munch	duch ess	cär to̤uch	at tach	check ers
punch	duch y	be seech	en rich	cher up
pinch	pĕrch er	im pēach	de ba̤uch	chill y

EXERCISE 133.

ch like *k.*

chăsm	chôrd	chō′ rist	schĕd′ ūle	är′ chīves
chā′ os	chrĭsm	chŏl er	schol ar	ī chor
chĕm ic	schōōl	chlo ric	schēme	păs chal
chem ist	chō′ rus	chlo rīne	schem er	ôr chis
chron ic	cho ric	cho ral	schōōn er	trō chee

EXERCISE 134.

āche	dĭs′ tich	är′ chon	är′ chi tect
chrome	eū nuch	mō cha	chăm o mile
är′ chil	mō loch	tēch ni cal	mech an ist
ĕch o	stŏm ach	scho las′ tic	är che tȳpe
ep och	mŏn arch	me chan ic	chăr ac ter

EXERCISE 135.

ch like *sh.*

çhāiṣe	çha grin′	çhĕv′ ron	çhĭv′ al ry
ma çhïne′	ga lŏche	chē mïse′	chär la tan
chi cāne	mus täche	chăp eau (ō)	chev a lïer′
cha rade	ba rouche	chat eau (ō)	chan de lier
cha made	de bouche	cham pā*g*ne	deb au chee

EXERCISE 136.

g hard, before *a*, *o*, *u*, *l*, and *r*.

gär′ land	gŏb′ bler	gŭm′ bo	glee′ ful	grăph′ ic
gāin say	gog gle	gun nel	glĭm mer	grā vy
gai ter	gos sip	gus to	glō ry	grēaṣ y
găl lop	gos pel	guz zle	glu cōse	greed y
gam mon	gôr mand	gun ny	glu ten	grīnd er

EXERCISE 137.

g hard, at the end of a word or a syllable not followed by *e*, *i*, or *y*; also, when doubled.

drăg′ on	brĭg′ and	răg′ ged	lĕg′ gin	dăg′ ger
big ot	rig or	leg ged	nog gin	brag ger
wag on	vig or	dog ged	pig gin	stag ger
flag on	wig gle	jog gle	wag gish	dig ger
drag on	smug gle	hig gle	slug gish	big ger

EXERCISE 138.

g usually soft, before *e*, *i*, or *y*.

ġĕn′ der	ġĭn′ ger	ġȳ′ rate	clĕr′ ġy	pĭl′ laġe
gest ure	gin seng	gy ral	sûr gy	band age
gen tīle	gib let	gȳm nast	dĭn gy	dam age
ger und	gib bet	gym nic	hinġ ing	im age
or ange	gī ant	con gēal′	strin ġent	ad age
man age	bro kage	en gāge	en lärge′	ar rānge′
ūṣ age	a gent	en cage	dis charge	de range
ge nus	ûr gent	pon gee	di vērge	en rage

EXERCISE 139.

prī' maġe	prĕs' aġe	sau' saġe	voy' aġe	vĕs' tiġe
rŭm mage	vis age	dō tage	cŏl lege	chal lenge
hom age	môrt gage	cŏt tage	al lēge'	gär bage
suf frage	cärt age	rav age	be siēge	dĕl uge
coŭr age	mĕs sage	sav age	o blīge	in dŭlge'

EXERCISE 140.

bădġe	wĕdġe	drŭdġe	bŭdġ' et	gŭd' ġeon
edge	midge	sludge	badg er	blud geon
hedge	ridge	sedge	lodg er	piġ eon
ledge	bridge	trudge	hedg er	wid ġeon
fledge	dodge	judge	pär tridge	sûr geon
pledge	lodge	dredge	car tridge	stur geon
sledge	budge	dīrge	dŭd geon	dŭn geon

EXERCISE 141.

ḡ sometimes hard, before *e*, *i*, and *y*.

ḡĕt	ḡīb'boŭs	ḡĭmp	be ḡĭn'	ḡeld' ing
get' ter	gid dy	gīrl	be get	gim bal
get ting	gift ed	girth	be gone	gim let
gew gaw	gig gle	gird	un gīrd	mug gy
gĭng ham	gild ing	gird' le	un gēar	fog gy

EXERCISE 142.

g silent, before *m* and *n* final; also, before *n* initial.

phlĕgm	con dīgn'	be nīgn'	as sīgn'	gnärl
deign	cam päign	de sign	im pūgn	gnăt
feign	ar raign	re sign	op pugn	gnash
reign	fŏr' eign	con sign	ex pugn	gnaw
sīgn	ma līgn'	ĕn' sign	ĭm prēgn	gno' mon

EXERCISE 143.

gh silent, before *t*, and at the end of a syllable.

hīgh	dīght	flīght	eight	bŏr' ōugh
nigh	hight	neigh	dōugh	thor ough
sigh	fight	weigh	though	fûr lough
thigh	light	weight	through	al though'
bight	blight	freight	haugh	in veigh

EXERCISE 144.

plī*gh*t	brī*gh*t	ca̤u*gh*t	bou*gh*t	da̤u*gh*′ ter
slight	fright	fraught	sought	slaugh ter
night	sight	naught	fought	bough (*bou*)
tight	wight	taught	thought	slough

EXERCISE 145.

gh like *f.*	*gh* like *f.*	*gh* like *k.*
läugh (*läf*)	slŏugh (*slŭf*)	hŏugh (*hŏk*)
laugh ter	clough	lough
rŏugh	e nŏugh′	shough
chough	côugh (*kawf*)	
tough	trough	*gh* like *p.*
sough	dráught (*draft*)	hie′ cŏugh (*hĭk kŭp*)

EXERCISE 146.

h silent, after *g*, after *r*, and after a vowel in the same syllable; also, at the beginning of some words.

g*h*ást	r*h*eṳm	ē′ phä*h*	*h*ĕrb
gha̤ut	rhīne	sĭr rah	hêir
ghōst	rhŏmb	rhṳ barb	hour
gho̤ul	rhȳme	ca tärrh′	hŏn′ or
g̃hee	rhȳthm	bûrgh′ er	hon est

EXERCISE 147.

k silent before *n*, and after *c*, in the same syllable.

*k*năb	*k*nāve	*k*new̃	*k*năc*k*	hăd′ doc*k*
knag	knēad	knīfe	crack	pad lock
knap	knee	knŏck	quack	wed lock
knit	kneel	knob	quick	ran sack
knot	knĕll	knōll	shock	bar rack

EXERCISE 148.

l sometimes silent, before *f, m, n, v, k, d, and c.*

hä*l*f	hä*l*ve	ca̤*l*k	co̤u*l*d	să*l*m′ on
calf	salve	chalk	would	äl mond
balm	qualm	stalk	should	fa̤*l* con er
calm	ba̤lk	walk	älms̱	em bälm′
palm	talk	auln	balm′ y	be calm

EXERCISE 149.

n, as in *man*, followed by *g* soft.

dān′ ġer	loun′ ġer	tăn′ ġent	im pĭnġe′	stĭn′ gy
man ger	plŭn ger	pun gent	un hinge	loun ger
ran ger	spŏn ger	loz enge	es trānge	crin ger
stran ger	spon gy	frin gy	re vĕnge	chan ger
tin ger	mān gy	ān gel	a venge	en gĭne

EXERCISE 150.

ng, as in *sing*, *singer*.

hăng	hăng′ er	hăng′ ing	kĭng′ ly	sīde′ long
wing	wing er	wing ing	spring y	sĭng-song
sing	sing er	sing ing	string y	ding-dong
ring	ring er	ring ing	där ling	strip ling
long	lŏng er*	long ing	wŏrld ling	hīre ling

EXERCISE 151.

n, like *ng*, before *c*, *g*, *k*, and *q*, as in *zinc*, *linger*.

răn′ cor	ăn′ ger	fĭn′ger	hŭn′ ger	jĭn′ gle
un cle	an gle	fun goŭs	lin ger	shin gle
con côrd	dan gle	clan gor	mŏn ger	tan gle
anch or	man gle	gan grēne	mon grel	bun gle
ink le	crink le	crank le	tink le	sprink le

EXERCISE 152.

lŏn′ ger*	hănk′ er	be thĭnk′	lăr′ ynx	thĭnk′ er
lon gest	thank ful	en link	ban quet	drink ing
stron ger	blank et	un link	anx ious	pink ish
stron gest	rank le	dĭn′ gle	con cōurse	twink le
yoŭn ger	an kle	tinct ūre	con gress	cinct ūre
youn gest	punct ure	span gle	san guine	junct ure

* Note that in such derivative words as *hang er*, *sing er*, *long er*, from *hang*, *sing*, and *long*, the *g* unites with the preceding *n* to represent the sound of *ng*. But in the comparative and superlative of the three words, *long*, *strong*, and *young*, and also in the words *diphthongal* and *triphthongal*, the *g* always takes its hard sound; as *longer*, *stronger*, *younger*.

EXERCISE 153.

n silent, after *m*, and *p* silent, before *n*, *s* and *t*.

dăm*n*	tĕm*p*t	cŏn tĕm*n*'	prŏm*p*t' ly	*p*sa̤l' ter y
hymn	prompt	con demn	at tempt'	psăl mo dy
limn	sŏl' emn	dis limn	con tempt	pneū măt' ic
pnyx	col umn	psälm' ist	sĕmp' stress	pneu mon ic
psälm	a̤u tumn	psa̤l ter	ptär mic	ptär' mi gan

EXERCISE 154.

s like *z*.

mū' s̱ic	dĭs̱' mal	nois̱' y	dĭs̱ cẽrn'	mĭs̱' e ry
mŏs lem	dāi sy	pa̤l sy	dis ēase	ris i ble
res in	drow sy	păn sy	dis ōwn	vis i ble
flim sy	ēas y	quin sy	dis sŏlve	mī ser ly
rōs y	pō sy	prōs y	dis ärm	ēas i ly

EXERCISE 155.

s like *sh*.

sṳre	sṳg' ar	as sṳre'	mĭs sion	sĕn' su al
sure ly	cĕn sure	in sure	man sion	as pẽr' sion
sure ty	ton sure	pĕn' sive	pas sion	e mer sion
sur est	press ure	scan sion	fis sion	a ver sion
su mac	fis sure	ten sion	vẽr sion	ex tĕn sion

EXERCISE 156.

s like *zh*.

fū' s̱ion	rās̱' ure	ō' s̱ier	clōs̱' ure	al lū' s̱ion
le sion	plĕas ure	ro sier	cro sier	col lu sion
vĭs ion	treas ure	ho sier	scĭs sure	con tu sion
trṳ sion	scĭs sion	mĕas ūre	ūs u ry	dif fu sion
suā sion	brā sier	lēi sure	us u al	in trṳ sion

EXERCISE 157.

t silent, after *s*, in words ending in *en* or *le*.

hās' *t*en	mois*t*' en	nes*t*' le	thĭs' *t*le	jŏs' *t*le
chas ten	ch̶rĭs ten	nest ling	whis tle	thros tle
fäst en	ŏft en	pes tle	bris tle	bŭs tle
lĭst en	soft en	tres tle	gris tle	hus tle
glis ten	căs tle	*w*res tle	nus tle	rus tle

EXERCISE 158.

t, after an accented syllable, and before *ia*, *ie*, or *io*, like *sh*.

pär′ tial	nā′ tion	pō′ tion	ạuc′ tion	sŭc′ tion
mar tial	ra tion	tôr tion	cau tion	cap tion
nŭp tial	lo tion	mĕn tion	trăc tion	fac tion
pā′ tient	mo tion	op tion	sec tion	frac tion
quo tient	no tion	ac tion	dic tion	fric tion

EXERCISE 159.

cre ā′ tion	e dĭ′ tion	fru ĭ′ tion	sal vā′ tion
ab lu tion	ad di tion	mō ni tion	plan ta tion
de vo tion	am bi tion	pär ti tion	mi gra tion
o ra tion	con di tion	ĭg ni tion	do na tion
for ma tion	con tri tion	po si tion	du ra tion

EXERCISE 160.

cre dĕn′ tial	sen tĕn′ tious	pro pĭ′ tious	vĭ′ ti ate
es sen tial	con ten tious	fac ti tious	ex pā′ ti ate
pru den tial	li cen tious	nu tri tious	ne go ti ate
po ten tial	in fec tious	se di tious	sub stăn ti ate
sol stĭ tial	fa cē tious	fla gi tious	in ĭ ti ate

EXERCISE 161.

th sharp, as in *thing*.

thēme	thĭn	thrŏb	thrĕat	thănk
thrive	thrush	thĭrd	thrīce	think
throne	thrum	thirst	thĭng	theft
thörn	thump	thrạll	throng	thick
thrăsh	thrust	thrĭll	thong	thrift

EXERCISE 162.

slŏth	nôrth	pĭth	mŏth	wôrth
bōth	hăth	smith	broth	hēath
ninth	snath	width	troth	heärth
päth	tenth	tilth	dȯth	dĕath
wạrmth	depth	plinth	mouth	breath

EXERCISE 163.

hĕalth	strĕngth	zē′ nith	ăn′ them	thŭn′ der
wealth	length	sab bath	thē ism	pā thos
stealth	fifth	nŏth ing	mĕth od	păn ther
south	filth	be trŏth′	ath lete	thresh ōld
ōath	fāith	for sōōth	thim ble	au thor

EXERCISE 164.

th flat, as in *thy.*

thēse	thăt	smōōth	sŏuth′ ern	be nēath′
thine	them	booth	fä ther	with draw
those	this	fĕath′ er	brŏth el	with hōld
thy	thus	leath er	lōath some	with stănd
thăn	they	heath er	făth om	thêre at

EXERCISE 165.

clōth′ ing	ŏth′ er	fär′ thing	tĕth′ er	fär′ ther
lōath ing	moth er	thêre fōre	hith er	fûr ther
thy sĕlf′	broth er	găth er	with er	wŏr thy
themselves	smoth er	lath er	thith er	blīthe some
thêre of	brĕth ren	rath er	fär thest	lithe some

EXERCISE 166.

w, consonant, as in *win.*

wab′ ble	wăg′ on	wĭck′ ed	wŏn′ der	wĭs′ dom
wad dle	wal let	wick er	wont ed	wŏn drous
waf fle	wal lop	wil lōw	work man	wĭn*d* rōw
wā fer	wal lōw	win dow	wōōd bīne	will ing
wa ġer	war ble	win now	wan ton	wish ful

EXERCISE 167.

dwĕll	swarm	swĭg	swan	swĭll
dwarf	swăg	swing	swĕrve	swāin
swāle	swam	swift	swap	sway
swine	sweep	swung	swamp	swēal
swarth	swĕpt	swab	swĕll	swōōn

EXERCISE 168.

swo͝op	twīne	twĭt	dwa̤rf' ish	swĭng' ing
swĕat	twĕlfth	twist	dwĭn dle	swag ġer
swinge	twelve	twāin	swel ter	swim mer
sweet	twig	twēak	swin dle	swin dler
twīce	twin	dwĕll ing	swĭn ish	swa̤l lōw

EXERCISE 169.

u, like *w* consonant after *g*, *s*, *q*, and *c* hard.

lăn̲' guaġe	lăn̲' guor	quăg' mīre	quī' et	lĭq' uid
lan guid	suā sive	qua̤r rel	quĭb ble	liq ue fy
lan guish	as suāġe'	quad rate	quick set	eq ui ty
lin guist	per suade	quā ver	quill ing	aq ue duct
lin gual	dis suade	que ry	quilt ing	cuï rass'
an guish	es quire	que rist	quid nun̲c	cui ṡīne

EXERCISE 170.

w silent.

*w*răck	*w*rĕnch	*w*rĭt	*w*hōle	*w*răn' gle
wrap	wretch	wrong	whōōp	wrig gle
wreck	wrist	wrīthe	swōrd	an swer
wren	wrēak	wrôth	wrĕnch	wrăth y
wrest	wreathe	wh̤o	wreck' er	tō ward
wrăth	wrŭng	whoṣe	wres tler	a wry'

EXERCISE 171.

w silent after a vowel in the same syllable.

lō*w*	blō*w*	bō*w*l	snō*w*	stō*w*
tow	own	crow	glow	growth
mow	blown	show	grow	throw
sow	flow	shown	grown	thrown
row	flown	slow	sown	ĕl' bōw

EXERCISE 172.

ăr' rō*w*	făl' lō*w*	hăr' rō*w*	mŏr' rō*w*	shăl' lō*w*
bil low	fel low	hol low	nar row	sor row
bor row	fol low	mar row	pil low	tal low
bûr row	hal low	mel low	sal low	wid ow
fur row	cal low	min now	shad ow	bel' low

EXERCISE 173.

wh pronounced like *hw*, as in *whack* (*hwack*).

whāle	whĕt	whĕlk	whĭp	whēat
whine	when	whelm	whim	wheel
whạt	whe̱y	whelp	whiff	wheeze
whăck	whạp	whence	which	whīrl
whang	whạ̈rf	whig	whīle	whêre

EXERCISE 174.

whāl′ er	whe̱y′ ey	whĭf′ fler	whĭsk′ er
whee dle	whĭm per	whis ky	whit lōw
wheez y	whin ny	whis per	whim ling
whĕr ry	whif fle	whīn ing	whig ḡish
wheth er	whif fet	whit ish	whīt ing

EXERCISE 175.

Sounds of *x*.

x like *ks*.	*x* like *gz*.	*x* like *gz*.	*x* like *ksh*.	*x* like *z*.
ex çĕl′	ex̱ ăct′	ex̱ ŭlt′	nŏx′ ious	xē′ bec
ex cept	ex empt	ex ūde	an̲x ious	xe riff
ex pend	ex ist	ex hôrt	flux ion	xȳs ter
ex cẽrpt	ex ạlt	ex hāle	flex ion	xiph oid
ex pert	ex ẽrt	ex hạ̈ust	sex u al	xan thic

EXERCISE 176.

y consonant, as in *you*, and *i* consonant as in *al′ ien.*

yĕl′ lōw	mĭn′ ion	āl′ ien	văl′ iant	pĭn′ ion
yon der	fus tian	fĭl ial	brill iant	on ion
hal yard	mill ion	bas tion	bill iards	pŏn iard
yēar ling	bun ion	bill ion	coll ier	span iel
lạ̈w yer	scall ion	bụll ion	cōurt ier	viz ier

EXERCISE 177.

z as in *zo̱ne*, and *z* like *zh*.

zā′ ny	zĕph′ yr	zĭg′ zag	lĭz′ ard	ăz′ ure
ze brȧ	zẽr dȧ	zin̲c ous	wiz ard	(*ăzh′ ure*)
ze bu	zē ro	diz zy	giz zard	az urn
ze bub	ze ta	fuz zy	haz ard	grā zier
ze nith	zeūg mȧ	ziz el	buz zard	sēi zure

SECTION X.

RULES FOR SPELLING.

RULE I.

Monosyllables ending in *f*, *l*, or *s*, immediately preceded by a single vowel, usually double the final letter.

EXERCISE 178.

råff	ŏff	fall	ĕll	ĭll
graff	buff	pall	tell	bill
clĭff	muff	tall	well	fill
skiff	snuff	stall	spell	hill
whiff	stuff	small	quell	pill

EXERCISE 179.

rĭll	thrĭll	skĭll	dŏll	lŭll
mill	trill	swill	loll	dull
sill	chill	trōll	poll	hull
frill	quill	stroll	rōll	null
drill	shrill	scroll	droll	mull

EXERCISE 180.

låss	mĕss	trĕss	lŏss	crŏss
pass	chess	stress	toss	gloss
class	cress	bless	boss	muss
brass	dress	kiss	moss	truss
grass	press	miss	floss	puss

EXCEPTIONS TO RULE I.

EXERCISE 181.

ĭf	găs	thĭs	săl, *salt.*
of (*ov*)	has	thus	bŭl, *a flounder.*
as	was	sŏl, *the sun.*	nul, *no; not any.*
is	his	sol, *a coin.*	pus, *morbid matter.*
us	yes	sōl, *note in music.*	clef, *key-note mark.*

RULE II.

Monosyllables ending in any other consonant than *f*, *l*, or *s*, preceded by a single vowel, do not double the final letter; thus, *top*, *dot*, *cox*, *whiz*. For numerous examples under this Rule, see pages 19 and 20.

EXCEPTIONS TO RULE II.

EXERCISE 182.

ăbb	ĭnn	fĭzz	jăgg, *a notch.*
add	mitt	fuzz	bigg, *kind of barley.*
ebb	plitt	buzz	butt, *a mark.*
egg	smitt	rudd	mumm, *to mask.*
odd	lamm	bĩrr	pärr, *kind of fish.*
ẽrr	wapp	shirr	scŏmm, *buffoon.*

RULE III.

Monosyllables ending with the *sound* of *k*, and in which *c* follows the vowel, usually take the letter *k* after the *c*.

EXERCISE 183.

băck	slăck	tăck	nĕck	pĭck
hack	smack	stack	peck	rick
lack	pack	beck	speck	sick
black	brack	deck	kick	tick
clack	crack	check	lick	wick
sack	track	fleck	nick	thick

EXERCISE 184.

clĭck	mŏck	flŏck	lŭck	plŭck
brick	pock	brock	duck	truck
trick	rock	crock	muck	struck
stick	sock	frock	tuck	stuck
chick	block	stock	buck	cluck
quick	clock	dock	suck	chuck

EXCEPTIONS TO RULE III.

EXERCISE 185.

tăle *a mineral.*	fĭsc, *treasury.*
zĭnc, *a metal.*	ôrc, *a kind of fish.*
äre, *part of a circle.*	sŏc, *tenant's privilege.*
săc, *bag.*	ploc, *mixture of hair and tar.*
lac, *a resinous substance.*	märc, *coin; refuse of pressed fruit.*
roc, *a large bird.*	

RULE IV.

Words of more than one syllable ending in *ic* or *iac*, that is, ending in the sound of *k*, do not, with the exception of the word, *der' rick*, assume the letter *k*.

EXERCISE 186.

stō' ic	trăg' ic	chrŏn' ic	ru' bric	frăn' tic
lu bric	log ic	ton ic	sphĕr ic	skep tic
frŏl ic	com ic	top ic	cen tric	cryp tic
rus tic	eth nic	trop ic	gas tric	styp tic
äre tic	clin ic	hec tic	clas sic	plas tic
cām bric	con ic	fab ric	an tic	caus tic

EXERCISE 187.

cär' di ac	lū' na tic	ăg' a ric	splĕn' e tic
ĭl i ac	plĕth o ric	Ar a bic	chol er ic
cē li ac	pol i tic	cath o lic	bish op ric
ma ni ac	r*h*et o ric	her e tic	cli mac' te ric
zo di ac	tûr mer ic	är se nic	a rith me tic

EXERCISE 188.

phĭ lĭp' pic	em pĭr' ic	ec çĕn' tric	lym phăt' ic
bar bar ic	his tor ic	fo ren sic	dra mat ic
çy lin dric	the at ric	in trin sic	prag mat ic
ge ner ic	e lec tric	ex trin sic	dog mat ic
hys ter ic	ob stet ric	em phat ic	ast*h* mat ic
syl lab ic	mor bif ic	spe cif ic	syn od ic
spas mod ic	pa cif ic	pro lif ic	som nif ic

EXERCISE 189.

rheṳ măt′ ic	ec stăt′ ic	ath lĕt′ ic	ar thrĭt′ ic
he pat ic	dĭ dac tic	e met ic	pleu rit ic
fa nat ic	pro phet ic	hĕr met ic	pe dant ic
qua̤d rat ic	pa thet ic	coş met ic	ġi gan tic
er rat ic	syn thet ic	mag net ic	ro man tic

EXERCISE 190.

a̤u thĕn′ tic	el lĭp′ tic	ġym năs′ tic	prog nŏs′ tic
eha ot ic	sar cas tic	mo nas tic	a cros tic
des pot ic	e las tic	fan tas tic	bal sam ic
ex̧ ot ic	seho las tic	ma jes tic	me ehan ic
e clip tic	ca thär tic	do mes tic	pul mon ic
ter rif ic	tho răç′ ic	ec cen tric	po et ic

RULE V.

Words of more than one syllable, in which *c*, in the ending, does not come after the vowels *i* or *ia*, terminate in *ck*.

EXERCISE 191.

ĭr′ rack	pēa′ cock	hĭll′ ock	hăm′ mock	hăs′ sock
bar rack	hăd dock	hem lock	ban nock	tus sock
car ack	pad dock	fet lock	pin nock	be deck′
ran sack	pad lock	cam mock	sham rock	un lock
ġim crack	wed lock	bu̥ll ock	cas sock	at tack
ġir rock	lin stock	wa̤r lock	fōre lock	a back
has sock	mat tock	fīre lock	bûr dock	un pack

EXCEPTIONS TO RULE V.

EXERCISE 192.

lĭm′ bec, *a still; an alembic.*
rē bec, *a musical instrument.*
xe bec (*ze bec*), *a kind of vessel or ship.*
hăv oc, *destruction.*
su̥′ mac (*shu mak*), *a plant or shrub.*
mā ni oc, *a tropical plant.*
săn da rac, *a sort of resin.*
a̤l ma nac, *a calendar.*

RULE VI.

In forming derivatives from words ending in *c*, the letter *k* is inserted before suffixes beginning with *e*, *i*, or *y*, to prevent the *c* from being sounded like *s*.

EXERCISE 193.

phy̆s' ic	trăf' fic	frŏl' ic	mĭm' ic
phys ick ed	traf fick er	frol ĭck ed	mim ick ed
phys ick ing	traf fick ing	frol ick ing	mim ick ing
col ic	gär lic	bĭv ouăc (-*wak*)	mim ick er
col ick y	gar lick y	biv ouack ed	biv ouack ing

RULE VII.

The final consonant of a monosyllable (*h* and *x* excepted), or of any word accented on the last syllable, if preceded by a single vowel, is doubled before a suffix beginning with a vowel.

EXERCISE 194.

băg	bĕg	con fẽr'	de fẽr'
bag' gage	beg' ging	con fer red	de fer red
bag ged	beg ged	con fer rec'	de fer ring
bag ging	beg gar	con fer' rer	de fer rer
bag gy	beg gar y	con fer ra ble	in fer red

EXERCISE 195.

cŏt	squab	pre fẽr'	re fẽr'
cot' ter	squab' by	pre fer red	re fer red
cot tage	squat	pre fer ring	re fer ring
cot ta ger	squat ting	pre fer rer	re fer rer
cot ta ged	squat ter	in fer ring	re fer' ri ble

EXERCISE 196.

stär	plăn	trans fẽr'	ex pĕl'
star' ry	plan' ner	trans fer red	ex pel led
star ri ness	plan ning	trans fer ring	ex pel ling
star red	clăn	trans fer rer	ex pel ler
star ring	clan nish	trans fer ri ble	ex pel la ble

EXERCISE 197.

găs	gŭm	com pĕl′	pro pĕl′
gas′ sy	gum′ ming	com pel led	pro pel led
gas sing	gum my	com pel ling	pro pel ling
quĭt*	gum mi er	com pel la ble	pro pel ler
quit ting	gum mi est	com pel la bly	dis pel ling

EXERCISE 198.

re bĕl′	be gĭn′	a bĕt′	ac quĭt′
re bel ling	be gin ning	a bet ted	ac quit ted
re bell ion	be gin ner	a bet ting	ac quit ting
re bell ious	be fog	a bet tor	ac quit tal
re bel ler	be fog ged	a bet tal	ac quit tance

EXCEPTIONS TO RULE VII.

EXERCISE 199.

găs′ es	from *gas.*	căb′ al ist	from *cabal′*
gaș e ous		cab a list′ ic	
gaș ē′ i ty		cab′ a lize	
gas′ i fy		cab al ișm	
con fer ence†	from *confer′.*		

EXERCISE 200.

dĕf′ er ent	from *defer′.*	rĕf′ er ence	from *refer′.*
def er ence		ref er a ble	
pref er ence	from *prefer′*	ref er ee′	
pref er a ble		in′ fer ence	from *infer′.*
pref er a bly		in fer a ble	

* The *u* in *quit* being equal to *w* consonant (*kwit*), forms no exception to the Rule.

† Notice that, in this word, the accent has been *thrown back* from the place it occupied in the primitive (*confer′*). When this change takes place, the rule seldom applies, and so arise exceptions such as most of those above. When, however, in forming derivatives, the accent is *thrown forward*, as in *eq′ ual, equal′ ity, for′ mal, for mal′ ity, an′ gel, an gel′ ic*, etc., the final letter is not generally doubled.

EXERCISE 201.

trăns′ fer ence trans fer′ a ble trans fer ee′	from *transfer′*.	sa līne′ sa līn ous săl′ i fy sal i fi a ble sal i fi cā′ tion	from *sal* (*salt*).
cha grĭn′ *e*d cha grin ing	from *chagrin′*.		

RULE VIII.

The final consonant of any word, if not immediately preceded by a single vowel, or not under the accent, remains single upon the addition of a suffix.

EXERCISE 202.

daub	need	brief	pĕt′ al
daub′ *e*d	need′ ed	brief′ er	pet al *e*d
daub ing	need ing	brief est	pet al ous
daub er	need y	vĭg or	pet al oid
daub y	heed ing	vig or ous	pet al ism

EXERCISE 203.

prŏf′ it	pī′ lot	ap păr′ el*	wŏŏl
prof it ed	pi lot ed	ap par el *e*d	wool′ en
prof it ing	pi lot age	băr′ rel	bī as
prof it a ble	bĕn e fit	bar rel *e*d	bi as *e*d
prof it a bly	ben e fit ed	bar rel ing	bi as ing

EXERCISE 204.

trăv′ el	căr′ ol	căv′ il	coun′ sel
trav el ing	car ol *e*d	cav il *e*d	coun sel *e*d
trav el er	car ol ing	cav il ing	coun sel ing
em bow′ el	căn′ çel	cav il er	coun sel or
em bow el *e*d	can cel *e*d	cav il ous	coun sel a ble
em bow el ing	can cel ing	cav il ous ly	counselorship

* Derivatives formed from primitives ending in *l*, or *p*, are by some written with the final letter double; thus, *traveller* instead of *traveler*, *worshipper* instead of *worshiper*, etc. This, however, is against the rule followed by Dr. Webster, which is founded on analogy, and ought to be observed.

EXERCISE 205.

dī′ al	dū′ el	en ăm′ el	ē′ qual
di al *ed*	du el ing	en am el *ed*	e qual *ed*
di al ing	du el ist	en am el ing	e qual ing
dĭ shĕv′ el	em păn′ el	en am el ar	e qual ize
di shev el *ed*	em pan el *ed*	en am el er	e qual iz *ed*
di shev el ing	em pan el ing	en am el ist	e qual′ i ty

EXERCISE 206.

găm′ bol	hătch′ el	jew′ el	kĭd′ nap
gam bol *ed*	hatch el *ed*	jew el *ed*	kid nap *ed*
gam bol ing	hatch el er	jew el er	kid nap ing
grav el	im pĕr′ il	kĕn nel	kid nap er
grav el *ed*	im per il *ed*	ken nel *ed*	lau rel
grav el ing	im per il ing	ken nel ing	lau rel *ed*

EXERCISE 207.

lā′ bel	lī′ bel	mär′ shal	mĕd′ al
la bel *ed*	li bel *ed*	mar shal *ed*	med al et
la bel ing	li bel ing	mar shal ing	med al ist
lĕv el	li bel er	mar vel	mod el
lev el ing	li bel ous	mar vel *ed*	mod el ing
lev el er	li bel ant	mar vel ous	mod el er

EXERCISE 208.

păn′ el	păr′ al lel	pĕn′ çil	pĕr′ il
pan el *ed*	par al lel *ed*	pen cil *ed*	per il *ed*
pan el ing	par al lel ing	pen cil ing	per il ing
pär çel	par al lel işm	pis tol	per il ous
par cel *ed*	par al lel ize	pis tol *ed*	per il ous ly
par cel ing	par al lel ĭs′ tic	pis tol ing	per il ous ness

EXERCISE 209.

vĭct′ *u*al	trăn′ quil	wôr′ ship	gŏs′ sip
vict ual *ed*	tran quil īze	wor ship *ed*	gos sip *ed*
vict ual ing	tran quil ized	wor ship ing	gos sip ing
vict ual er	nov el	wor ship er	met al
vī ol	nov el ist	găl lop	met al *ed*
vi ol is′ tic	nov el ize	gal lop ing	met al ing

EXCEPTIONS TO RULE VIII.

EXERCISE 210.

hŭm′ bug ged hum bug ging hum bug ger hum bug ger y	from *hŭmbug.*	mĕt′ al loid met al list met al lize met al līne me tăl′ lic	from *metal.*
per i wig ged per i wig ging	from *periwig.*	me dal lic	from *medal.*

EXERCISE 211.

crȳs′ tal līne crys tal loid crys tal līze crys tal liz ed crys tal liz a ble* crys tal li zā′ tion	from *crystal.*	chȧn′ cel lor chan cel lor ship	from *chancel.*
		tran quĭl′ li ty	*tranquil.*
		tȳr′ an ny tyr an nīze tȳ răn′ nic	from *tyran.*†

RULE IX.

Words ending in a double consonant usually retain both letters upon receiving a suffix.

EXERCISE 212.

ădd	ĕbb	ẽrr	mŭmm
add′ ed	ebb′ ed	err′ ed	mumm′ ed
add ing	ebb ing	err ing	mumm ing
re mĭss′	egg	er rant	mum mer
re miss ness	egg er y	er răt′ ic	mum mer y

EXERCISE 213.

quȧff	whĭff	tăr′ iff	stĭff
quaff′ ed	whiff′ ed	tar iff ed	stiff er
quaff ing	whiff ing	bluff	stiff est
bŭzz	whif fet	bluff ness	stiff en
buzz ed	cliff	sher iff	stiff ly
buzz ing	cliff y	sher iff al ty	stiff ness

* See also, *cancellation*, p. 153. † Old form for *tyrant.*

EXERCISE 214.

scŏff	dŏff	hŭff	grŭff
scoff' *e*d	doff' *e*d	huff' y	gruff' ly
scoff ing	doff ing	huff i ness	gruff ness
scoff er	cuff	huff ish	gruff er
scoff er y	cuff *e*d	huff ish ly	sqṳall
scoff ing ly	cuff ing	huff er	squall y

EXERCISE 215.

sma̤ll	ap pa̤ll'	in stĭll'	thra̤ll
small' er	ap pall *e*d	in still ing	thrall' *e*d
small est	ap pall ing	in still ment	thrall dom
small ness	ap pall ing ly	in still er	thrall ing
small ish	ap pall ment	in stil lā' tion	thrall-less*

EXERCISE 216.

drōll	påss	lĕss	in thra̤ll'
droll' er	pass' ing	less' *e*n	in thrall ment
droll er y	pass er	bliss	in sta̤ll
droll ish	pass a ble	bliss ful	in stall ment
droll ing ly	păs sage	bliss less	in stal lā' tion

EXERCISE 217.

smĕll	chĭll	rōll	stĭll
smell'-less	chill' ing	roll' er	still' er
hill	chill ness	roll ing	still est
hill y	chill y	roll *e*d	still ness
hill ock	chill i ness	roll a ble	still y

EXERCISE 218.

wĭll	skĭll	dŭll	fu̇ll
will' ful	skill' ful	dull' ness	full' ness
will ing	skill ful ly	dull ish	ga̤ll
will ing ness	skill *e*d	bell	gall ing
will er	skill-less	bell-less	gall-less

* Words ending in *ll*, upon taking the suffix *less*, either insert a hyphen (-), as in *thrall-less*, or drop one *l*, and so become exceptions to the rule; thus, *bel-less*, for *bell-less*.

EXCEPTIONS TO RULE IX.

EXERCISE 219.

pon tĭf' ic		ĭl' ly*		*ill*
pon tif ic al		dul ly		*dull*
pon tif ic al ly	from *pontiff.*	ful ly	from	*full*
pon tif ic ate		shril ly		*shrill*
pon ti fĭ' cial		smal ly		*small*

RULE X.

Words ending with *e* silent commonly drop the *e* upon taking a suffix beginning with a vowel.

EXERCISE 220.

dōte	blāme	blas phēme'	brŏnze
dōt' ed	blām' ed	blas phem ed	bronz' ing
dot ing	blam ing	blas phem er	bronz ĭne
do tard	blam er	blăs' phe mous	bronz ist
do tage	blam a ble	blas phe my	bronz y

EXERCISE 221.

ca rouse'	clōse	vĭrt' ūe	stăt' ūe
ca rous ing	clos' ing	virt u al	stat u ing
ca rous er	clos er	virt u al ly	stat u a ry
ca rous al	clos ure	virt u ous	stat u ĕtte'
ca rous ing ly	clŏs et	virt u ous ly	stat u esq*ue*

EXERCISE 222.

r*h*ȳme	brāve	sāne	stȳle
rhȳm' er	brāv' er	săn' i ty	stȳl' ish
rhym ist	brav est	san i ta ry	shade
rhym ic	brav er y	san a tive	shad y
rhym er y	bra vā' do	san a to ry	shad i ness

* The second *l*, in each of these words, *ill, dull, full, shrill, small*, is left out, as is plain, to prevent the *tripling* of that letter in the middle of a word; otherwise they would have to be written *ill-ly, dull-ly, full-ly, shrill-ly*, and *small-ly*, as in the case of *skill-less*, &c. See note, page 66.

EXERCISE 223.

vălve	zōne	lȳ′ ing*	from	lie
valv′ ate	zōn′ ūle	ty ing		tie
valv ūle	zon u lar	vy ing		vie
valv u lar	zo nar	hy ing		hie
up hēave′	be hāve′	dy ing		die
up heav al	be hav ior	ey ing		eye

EXCEPTIONS TO RULE X.

EXERCISE 224.

pēaçe	sẽr′ vĭçe	pro nounçe′	chärġe
peace′ a ble	ser vice a ble	pro nounce a ble	charge′ a ble
trāçe	dĭ vōrçe′	en tīçe	dăm aġe
trace a ble	di vorce a ble	en tice a ble	dam age a ble
piērçe	en fōrçe	nō′ tīce	man aġe
pierce a ble	en force a ble	no tice a ble	man age a ble

EXERCISE 225.

chăl′ lenġe	chānġe	out′ rāġe	dȳe′ ing‡
chal lenge a ble	change′ a ble	out rā′ ġeous	sĭnġe ing
măr riaġe	lŏdġe	ad văn taġe	tinġe ing
mar riage a ble	lodge a ble	ad van tā′ ġeous	swinġe ing
voy aġe	coŭr aġe	môrt′ gaġe	sprinġe ing
voy age a ble	cou rā′ ġeous	mort gage or′†	mīle aġe

EXERCISE 226.

līne	see	a gree′	de cree′
lĭn′ e al	see′ ing	a gree a ble	de cree a ble
lin e aġe	flee	ra zee	hōe
lin e ar	flee ing	ra ze ed	hoe ing
lin e ate	fric as see′	ra zee ing	toe
con′ gē	fric as see ing	vĭ se (vē zā)	toe ing
con ge ed	free	vi se ed	shoe
con ge ing	free′ ing	vi se ing	shoe ing

* Note that in *lying, tying, vying, hying, dying,* (from *die*), after the *e* is dropped according to rule, the *i* preceding is changed into *y* to prevent the doubling of *i* in the middle of a word.

† The *e* after *c* and *g*, in all these examples, is retained in order to preserve the soft sounds of these letters.

‡ The *e*, in *dyeing, tingeing, swingeing, singeing, springeing,* serves to distinguish these words from *dying* (to expire), tinging, swinging, etc.

RULE XI.

Words ending with *e* silent, retain the *e* before a suffix beginning with a consonant.

EXERCISE 227.

sāfe	dūke	free	mĕd′ dle
safe′ ty	duke′ dom	free′ ly	med dle some
pale	dȯve	house	nīne
pale ness	dove let	house less	nine ty
flame	sŭp ple	mōle	ạu stēre′
flame let	sup ple ness	mole cule	au stere ly
re quīre′	hōme	prĭnce	con dōle
re quire ment	home ly	prince dom	con dole ment
rĕs′ pīte	lone	līke	trīte
res pite less	lone some	like ness	trite′ ly

EXCEPTIONS TO RULE XI.

EXERCISE 228.

dūe	*w*hōle	nûrse	lŏdġe
du′ ly	whol′ ly	nurs′ ling	lodg′ ment
trụe	ạwe	är′ gūe	a brĭdġe′
tru ly	aw ful	ar gu ment	a bridg ment
ac crụe′	wīṣe	judġe	ac *k*no*w*l′ edġe
ac crụ ment	wĭs dom	judg ment	ac *k*no*w*l edg ment

RULE XII.

Words ending with *y*, preceded by a consonant, on receiving a suffix, commonly change the *y* into *i*.

EXERCISE 229.

bŏd′ y	mẽr′ çy	stŭd′ y	vā′ ry
bod i ly	mer ci ful	stud ied	va ri ous
bod ies	mer ci less	stud i er	va ri a ble
gid dy	sạu çy	stū′ di ous	va ri ā′ tion
gid di ness	sau ci ly	stu di ous ly	va rī′ e ty

EXERCISE 230.

căr′ ry	hōar′ y	nā′ vy	mĕl′ o dy
car ried	hoar i ness	na vies	mel o dies
car ries	dī a ry	dĭt ty	dȳ nas ty
car riage	di a rist	dit ties	dy nas ties
car ri er	di ā′ ri al	çit y	cru el ty
car ri a ble	di a ri an	cit ies	cru el ties

EXCEPTIONS TO RULE XII.

EXERCISE 231.

shȳ	slȳ	drȳ	sprȳ
shy′ er	sly′ er	dri′ er*	spry′ er
shy est	sly est	dri est	spry est
shy ly	sly ly	dry ly	*w*rȳ
shy ness	sly ness	dry ness	wrȳ ness

EXERCISE 232.

bā′by	sure′ ty	pĭt′ y	pū′ ri ty
ba by hood	sure ty ship	pit e ous	pu ri tan
ba by ship	dū ty	plen ty	chăr i ty
la dy	du te ous*	plen te ous	char i ta ble
la dy kin	boun ty	beaū ty	ver i ty
la dy ship	boun te ous	beau te ous	ver i ta ble

RULE XIII.

The final *y* when preceded by a vowel, or when coming before a suffix beginning with the letter *i*, remains unchanged.

EXERCISE 233.

kēy	jŏck′ ey	mon′ ey	monk′ ey
keys	jock eys	mon eys	monk eys
key′ age	jock ey ed	mon ey ed	monk ey ism
lăck ey	jock ey ing	mon ey less	vŏl ley
lack eys	jock ey ism	mon ey er	vol leys
lack ey ing	jock ey ship	mon ey age	vol ley ed

* Note that *drier* and *driest* follow the rule, and that *duty, pity, plenty, bounty,* and *beauty,* change *y* final into *e*; while in *puritan,* and *charitable,* as in some similar cases, the *y* is simply omitted.

EXERCISE 234.

văl′ ley	pär′ ley	joŭr′ ney	sur vey′
val leys	par ley ing	jour ney ed	sur vey ing
al ley	hŏn ey	jour ney ing	sur vey al
al leys	hon ey ed	jour ney er	sur vey or
gal ley	hăck ney	at tor′ ney	cau′ sey
gal leys	hack ney ed	at tor neys	cau sey ed

EXERCISE 235.

clāy	de coy′	ĕn′ vy	cŭl′ ly
clay′ ish	de coy ing	en vy ing	cul ly ism
clay ey	de coy ed	glō ry	spȳ
whey	en joy	glo ry ing	spy ism
whey ish	en joy ing	vā ry	dis plāy′
whey ey	en joy ment	va ry ing	dis play ed

EXCEPTIONS TO RULE XIII.

EXERCISE 236.

lāid, paid, mis lāid′, re paid, un paid	from	*lay.* *pay.*	stāid, slain, said, saith, dai′ ly	from	*stay.* *slay.* *say.* *day.*

RULE XIV.

Words ending in *f* or *fe* commonly change the *f* into *v* upon receiving a suffix beginning with a vowel.

EXERCISE 237.

griēf	thiēf	sāfe	be liēf′
grieve	thiev′ ing	save	be lieve
griev′ ing	thiev ish	sav′ ed	be liev ed
griev ance	thiev ish ness	sav ing	be liev ing
griev ous	thiev ish ly	sav ing ly	be liev er
griev a ble	thiev er y	sav er	be liev a ble

EXCEPTIONS TO RULE XIV.

EXERCISE 238.

dĕaf	briēf	gŭlf	dwarf
deaf′ en	brief′ er	gulf′ y	dwarf′ ish
ōaf	wolf	tûrf	dwarf ish ness
oaf ish	wolf ish	turf y	dwarf *e*d
lēaf	ĕlf	turf *e*d	dwarf ing
leaf y	elf ish	turf ing	sāfe
chiēf	self	shĕlf	saf er
chief est	self ish	shelf y	saf est

RULE XV.

SPELLING OF PLURALS.

Nouns ending in a *sound* that will unite with that of *s*, form the plural by adding *s* only; in other cases, the plural is regularly formed by adding *es*.

EXERCISE 239.

SINGULAR.	PLURAL IN S.	SINGULAR.	PLURAL IN ES.
cŏm′ ma	cŏm′ mas	lāçe	lāç′ es
cob web	cob webs	ĕdġe	ĕdġ es
pan ic	pan ics	niche	nich es
aç id	aç ids	wish	wish es
lap dog	lap dogs	lens	lens es
bāil iff	bāil iffs	glȧss	glȧss es
fū see′	fu sees′	çhāise	chāis es

EXERCISE 240.

stŏm′ ach	stŏm′ achs	côrpse	côrps′ es
mŭf tĭ	muf tis	nûrse	nûrs es
der rick	der ricks	blāze	blāz es
ras cal	ras cals	bŏx	bŏx es
a lärm′	a lärms′	buzz	buzz es
Gẽr′ man	Gẽr′ mans	cĩr cus	cĩr cus es
tȳ ro	tȳ ros	găl′ lōws	găl lōws es
bam bōō′	bam bōōs′	sum mons	sum mons es

EXCEPTIONS TO RULE XV.

EXERCISE 241.

SINGULAR.	PLURAL.	SINGULAR.	PLURAL.
nō	noes̤	brā′ vo	brā′ voes̤
hē′ ro	hē′ roes	mŏt to	mŏt toes
ne gro	ne groes	grot to	grot toes
ĕch o	ĕch oes	bil bo	bil boes
cär go	cär goes	bū bo	bū boes
po tā′ to	po tā′ toes	căl i co	căl i coes
vol ca no	vol ca noes	pōr ti co	pōr ti coes
em bär go	em bär goes	tor nā′ do	tor nā′ does
bŭf′ fä lo	bŭf′ fä loes	tor pe do	tor pe does
mu lăt′ to	mu lăt′ toes	vi ra go	vi ra goes
man i fĕs′ to	man i fĕs′ toes	in nu ĕn′do	in nu ĕn′ does
mag nif′ i co	mag nif′ i coes	pec ca dil lo	pec ca dil loes*

EXERCISE 242.

shēaf	shēaves̤†	ĕlf	ĕlves̤
leaf	leaves	shelf	shelves
lōaf	lōaves	self	selves
beef	beeves	wọlf	wọlves
thiēf	thiēves	līfe	līves
cä*l*f	cä*l*ves	wife	wives
ha*l*f	ha*l*ves	*k*nife	*k*nives

EXERCISE 243.

wha̤rf	{ wha̤rfs	hŏb′ by	hŏb′ bies̤‡
	{ wharves̤	bŏd y	bŏd ies
stȧff	{ stȧffs	bo͞o by	bo͞o bies
	{ stāves	mẽr çy	mẽr çies
răb′ bĭ	{ răb′ bĭs	trō phy	trō phies
	{ rab bies	wór thy	wór thies
ăl′ ka lĭ	{ ăl′ ka lĭs	bụl ly	bụl lies
	{ al ka lies	al lȳ′	al līes′

* The exceptions ending in *o*, it will be observed, are words in which the *o* is preceded by a *consonant.* Few in which that is the case, follow the rule; but, among them are some in very general use, as *halo, halos; quarto, quartos; salvo, salvos; junto, juntos; canto, cantos; octavo, octavos; memento, mementos.*

† For the change of *f* into *v* in these examples, see Rule XIV.

‡ For the change of *y* into *i* in forming these plurals, see Rule XII.

EXERCISE 244.

SINGULAR.	PLURAL.	SINGULAR.	PLURAL.
man	men	bróth′er	bróth′ers breth ren
yeō′ man	yeō′ men		
ŏx	ŏx en	pēa	pēas pease
dīe	dīes diçe	pĕn′ ny	pĕn′ nies pençe
chīld	chĭl′ dren		
fo͝ot	feet	mouse	mīçe
to͞oth	teeth	dôr′ mouse	dôr′ mīce
go͞ose	geese	wọm an	wom en
louse	līçe	fōe man	fōe men

EXERCISE 245.

bā′ sis*	bā′ sēs	ar cā′ num	ar cā′ na
cri sis	cri sēs	er ra tum	er ra ta
da tum	da ta	el lĭp sis	el lĭp sēs
fo cus	fo cī	syn op sis	syn op sēs
ma gus	ma ġī	a lum nus	a lum nī
pha sis	pha sēs	nĕb′ u la	nĕb′ u læ
the sis	the sēs	stim u lus	stim u lī
ăx is	ăx ēs	tēr mi nus	tēr mi nī
ros trum	ros tra	ver te bra	ver te bræ
lär va	lär væ	a năl′ y sis	a năl′ y sēs

EXERCISE 246.

fō′ cus	fō′ cus es fo ci	rā′ di us	rā′ di us es ra di ī
sĕr aph	sĕr aphs sĕr a phim	nu cle us	nu cle us es nu cle ī
in dex	in′ dex es in di cēs	en cō′ mi um	en cō′ mi ums en co mi a
ban dit	ban dits ban dit′ ti	ġym na si um	ġym na si ums gym na si a
mē′ di um	mē′ di ums me di a	au tŏm a ton	au tŏm a tons au tom a ta
ge ni us	ge ni us es ge ni ī	phe nom e non	phe nom e nons phe nom e na

* Exercises 245 and 246 consist entirely of words from foreign languages, which, in English, retain the foreign forms of the plural. Some of them, however, have, also, the regular English form.

RULE XVI.

Compound words usually retain the spelling proper to the simple words composing them.

EXERCISE 247.

blūe′ bell*	brīde′ gro͞om	rĕd′ top	hīgh′ way
bo͝ok store	night mare	red wing	găng way
book worm	night shade	red bird	päth way
brĕast pin	plāy thing	black bird	bīrth day
breast plate	play *w*right	blūe bird	do͞omş day

EXERCISE 248.

stär′ light	hīgh′ land	blăck′ board	whĕt′ stone
mo͞on light	hĕad land	ship board	mill stone
dāy light	lōw land	fo͝ot fall	lōad stone
blŏck hĕad	dŏg star	foot man	brow bēat
round head	vīne yard	foot stool	chûrch man

EXERCISE 249.

cōach′ man	whōle′ sale	māin′ sail	no͞on′ tide
bĕd stĕad	steerş mate	main spring	grănd sire
mĕr maid	hĕad long	scâre crow	wâre house
slĭp shod	līve long	bōw string	ēar ache
tûrn pike	bon fire	brĕak fast	to͞oth ache

EXERCISE 250.

beâr′ş′-foot	nīght′-fall	rĕd′-hot	do͞or′-way
blūe-fish	oil-man	cat-bird	pay-day
bo͝ok-case	plāy-book	snōw-bird	rōw-boat
brīde-cake	pŭmp-stock	rīce-bird	stēam-boat
bride's-maid	pûrse-proud	pine-tree	găs-light

* The two parts of a permanent compound are usually written together as one word; as *breastpin;* in other cases they are connected by a hyphen, as in *door-way, book-case.* When the first part of the compound is a noun in the Possessive Case, the sign (') of possession is mostly omitted, thus, *bondsman,* not *bond'sman.* Sometimes, also, the *s* is dropped, as in *bondman.* For the accentuation of compounds, see p. 80.

EXERCISE 251.

bŭlk′-head	bāse′-ball	stēam′-ship	chûrch′-yard
tan-yard	fĩrst-born	dĕath-bed	clōthes-horse
dāy-star	foot-hold	bōw-knot	home-bred
sound-board	mīle-stone	căt's-päw	free-will
âir-built	stär-fish	chōke-peâr	Māy-pole

EXERCISE 252.

clŭb′-foot	tŏp′-knot	ĕdge′-tool	shĭp′-load
whip-lash	snōw-drop	pack-thread	bank-note
hīde-bound	māin-stay	tell-tale	ȧrm-châir
fire-work	brain-sick	heärt-ache	bāil-bond
hâir-cloth	sea-gull	grȧss-plot	bär-maid

SECTION XI.

ACCENTUATION OF CERTAIN CLASSES OF WORDS.

Words of twó or more syllables, ending in *ee* and *ose* usually have the accent on the last syllable.*

EXERCISE 253.

ee	*ee*	*ose*	*ose*
trust ee′	leg a tee′	vĕr bōse′	cū′ mu lose
grant ee	ref er ee	mor bose	ar e nose
les see	as sign ee	jo cose	ad i pose
do nee	ref u gee	mo rose	op er ose
set tee	ab sen tee	cri nose	côr ti cose
tou pee	dev o tee	ve nose	cō ma tose

* Those ending in *ose*, of *three* syllables, however, are now by the best and most recent authorities accented on the *first* syllable; the last syllable being still distinguished by a sort of secondary accent.

Words ending in *ic* and *ics* usually have the accent on the last syllable but one.*

EXERCISE 254.

ic	*ic*	*ic*	*ics*
he rō′ ic	re pŭb′ lic	syl lăb′ ic	ĕth′ ics
har mŏn ic	an gel ic	syn od ic	op tics
la con ic	po lem ic	pa cif ic	stat ics
bo tan ic	spe cif ic	le thär gic	me chăn′ ics
sa tan ic	pro lif ic	mo sā ic	pneū mat ics
se raph ic	tĕr rif ic	pro sa ic	hys ter ics

Words ending in *sion* and *tion* have the accent on the last syllable but one.†

EXERCISE 255.

sion	*sion* and *tion.*	*tion*
ex cûr′ sion	sup prĕs′ sion	ad o rā′ tion
con fĕs sion	con ces sion	af fec ta tion
de clen sion	com mis sion	ob li ga tion
di men sion	ad dĭ tion	com bi na tion
per vẽr sion	con di tion	con sti tu tion
in ver sion	frụ i tion	av o ca tion

Words with the endings, *cate*, *date*, *gate*, *fy*, *tude*, and *ty*, preceded by a vowel, usually have the accent on the last syllable but two.

EXERCISE 256.

cate and *date*	*gate* and *fy*	*tude* and *ty*
dĕp′ re cate	dĕl′ e gate	lăt′ i tude
pred i cate	ag gre gate	am pli tude
ed u cate	nav i gate	fôr ti tude
can di date	rar e fy	dĕp u ty
an te date	mod i fy	lib er ty
liq ui date	jus ti fy	pū ber ty

* For some exceptions to this, see Exercise 187, page 59.

† For the sound of *si* and *ti* in these terminations, see page 10.

Words of more than two syllables, ending *ia*, *iac*, *ial*, *ian*, *eous*, and *ious*, have the accent on the syllable immediately before these terminations.

EXERCISE 257.

ia	*iac*	*ial*
mā′ ni a	Sȳr′ i ac	lā′ bi al
sco ri a	sal mi ac	pre di al
däh li a	hē li ac	me ni al
hēr ni a	the ri ac	ve ni al
re gā′ li a	e lē′ gi ac	ge ni al
mĭ lĭ tia	de mo ni ac	côr di al
lō bē li a	sym po ṣi ac	sē ri al

EXERCISE 258.

ian	*eous*	*ious*
guärd′ i an	hĭd′ e ous	grā′ cious
rŭf fian	ig ne ous	spa cious
tēr tian	pit e ous	te di ous
stȳġ i an	dū te ous	o di ous
ple bē′ ian	nau se ous	con tā′ gious
me rĭd i an	hēr bā′ ceous	pre co cious
co mē di an	crus ta ceous	me lo di ous
tra ge di an	po ma ceous	fe lo ni ous

Words ending in *acal* and *ical* have the accent on the syllable immediately before these terminations.

EXERCISE 259.

acal	*ical*	*ical*
he lī′ ac al	mĕd′ ic al	mo närch′ ic al
cär di ac al	mag ic al	en cȳc lic al
ma ni ac al	log ic al	sym bol ic al
the ri ac al	graph ic al	pe ri ŏd′ ic al
zo di ac al	com ic al	ge o graph ic al
de mo ni′ ac al	stō ic al	di a bol ic al
am mo ni ac al	cu bic al	non sens ic al
el e gi ac al	trăg ic al	syn od ic al

Words ending in *eal*, *ean*, and *eum* are accented, some of them on the penult, or the last syllable but one, and some on the antepenult, or last syllable but two.

EXERCISE 260.

Accent on the penult.	*Accent on the penult.*
i dē′ al	hy men ē′ al
un re al	em py re an
pyg me an	At lan te an
Le the an	Eū ro pe an
mu ṣe um	col os se um
ly ce um	mau so le um

EXERCISE 261.

Accent on the antepenult.	*Accent on the antepenult.*
lĭn′ e al	em pȳr′ e al
bō re al	ce ru le an
ce re al	nec tā re an
lăc te al	pe tro le um
os se an	hy per bō′ re an
ôr de al	Ep i cu re an
ar bō′ re al	Her cu la ne an
cor po re al	sub ter ra ne an

Words with the following endings,* have the accent on the last syllable but two.

EXERCISE 262.

de mŏc′ ra cy	my thŏl′ o gy	an tĭph′ o ny
som nif er ous	so lil o quy	mi cros co py
cir cum flu ent	lo gom a chy	a pos tro pho
di ag o nal	po lym a thy	a nat o my
coṣ mog o ny	ba rom e ter	phi los o phy
ge og ra pher	ge om e try	mo not o ny
as trol o ger	e con o my	bel lig er ous
phĭ lol o gist	o vip a rous	ig niv o mous
su pĕr flu ous	an tip a thy	cär niv o rous

* That is, words ending in *cracy*, *ferous*, *fluent*, *gonal*, *gony*, *grapher*, etc.

Compound words have the accent on the *first*, or *specifying* term.

EXERCISE 263.

blīnd' man	ĭnk' stand	märks' man	hănd' spīke
name sake	hen bane	wórk man	hôrn pipe
brĭm stone	rats bane	lūke warm	wĭnd mill
broad side	stātes man	lănd lord	milk maid
broad sword	sports man	land mark	trādes man
green gage	bīrd man	linch pin	keep sake
green horn	*wrĭst* band	hedge hog	keel man
green sward	grand child	cat mint	house hold
brāke man	hand maid	hang man	skĭn flint

Words in which a change of accent, involves a change of meaning.

EXERCISE 264.

ăb' sent, *not present.*	ab sĕnt', *to keep away.*
ab stract, *a part; summary.*	ab stract, *to take away.*
ac cent, *stress of voice.*	ac cent, *to put under accent.*
af fix, *something added.*	af fix, *to add something.*
aug ment, *increase.*	aug ment, *to increase.*
Au gust, *the eighth month.*	au gust, *grand; stately.*
cĕm ent, *that which unites.*	ce mĕnt, *to unite with cement.*
col league, *partner; associate.*	col lēague, *to join with.*
col lect, *short prayer.*	col lĕct, *to gather together.*
com pact, *a contract.*	com pact, *close; to pack.*

EXERCISE 265.

cŏm' plot, *a plotting together.*	com plŏt', *to plot together.*
com pound, *a mixture.*	com pound, *to mix; mingle*
com press, *a linen pad.*	com prĕss, *to press together.*
con cert, *harmony.*	con cĕrt, *to contrive together.*
con crete, *united in growth.*	con crēte, *to unite, or coalesce.*
con duct, *behavior; manners.*	con dŭct, *to lead; manage.*
con fect, *a sweatmeat.*	con fect, *to prepare sweetmeats.*
con fine, *a border, or limit.*	con fīne, *to limit; restrain.*
con flict, *a contest; struggle.*	con flĭct, *to strike together.*

EXERCISE 266.

cŏn′ jŭre, *to practice sorcery.*	con jūre′, *to enjoin solemnly.*
cŏm post, *mixture for manure.*	com pōst, *to manure with compost.*
con serve, *a sweatmeat.*	con sẽrve, *to preserve.*
con sort, *a wife or husband.*	con sôrt, *to associate; unite.*
con test, *a strife; struggle.*	con tĕst, *to contend.*
con tract, *a bargain.*	con tract, *to draw together.*
con trast, *opposition.*	con trast, *to put in contrast.*
con vent, *cloister.*	con vent, *to meet together.*
con verse, *discourse.*	con vẽrse, *to talk with.*
cŏn vert, *one converted.*	con vert, *to turn; to change.*
con vict, *one found guilty.*	con vĭct, *to prove one guilty.*
con voy, *an escort for defense.*	con voy, *to escort for defense.*

EXERCISE 267.

dĕṣ′ ert, *a waste; wilderness.*	de ṣẽrt′, *to forsake; abandon.*
des cant, *a song; melody.*	des cănt, *to discourse at large.*
dī gest, *a body of laws.*	di gest, *to prepare; arrange.*
dĭs count, *deduction.*	dis count, *to deduct from.*
es cort, *guard; attendant.*	es côrt, *to attend; guard.*
eș say, *an attempt; treatise.*	es sāy, *to try; attempt.*
ex port, *goods sent abroad.*	ex pōrt, *to send goods abroad.*
ex tract, *that taken out.*	ex trăct, *to take or draw out.*
fẽr ment, *internal motion.*	fer ment, *to cause ferment.*
fōre cȧst, *foresight.*	fore cȧst, *to plan beforehand.*

EXERCISE 268.

fōre′ taste, *taste beforehand.*	fore tāste′, *enjoy beforehand.*
fre quent, *often.*	fre quĕnt, *to visit often.*
găl lant, *daring; high-spirited.*	gal lant, *attentive to ladies.*
im pact, *control by touch.*	im pact, *to press firmly.*
im port, *goods from abroad.*	im pōrt, *to bring in.*
im press, *mark; image.*	im prĕss, *to mark, or stamp.*
in cense, *odor from spices.*	in cense, *to fire; provoke.*
in crēase, *augment.*	in crēase, *to augment.*
in lay, *that which is inlaid.*	in lāy, *insert for ornament.*
in stinct, *inward impulse.*	in stĭnct, *urged from within.*
in sult, *affront; abuse.*	in sult, *to affront; abuse.*
min ute (*min it*), *sixty seconds.*	mi nūte, *very small.*

EXERCISE 269.

ŏb′ ject, *that under notice.*	ob jĕct′, *to oppose; set before.*
out law, *one excluded from the benefit of law.*	out la̤w, *to deprive of the benefit of law.*
pĕr fect, *complete.*	per fĕct, *to complete.*
per fume, *scent; fragrance.*	per fūme, *to scent.*
per mit, *warrant.*	per mĭt, *to allow.*
per vert, *one misled.*	per vĕrt, *to mislead.*
prē fix, *what is prefixed.*	pre fĭx, *to fix before.*
pre lude, *introduction.*	pre lūde, *to introduce.*
prĕm ise, *ground of argument.*	pre mi̱se, *state beforehand.*

EXERCISE 270.

prē′ sage, *omen.*	pre sāge′, *to give omens.*
prĕs ent, *not absent; a gift.*	pre sĕnt, *to offer.*
prod uce, *what is produced.*	pro dūce, *to bring forth.*
prog ress, *advance.*	pro grĕss, *to advance.*
proj ect, *plan; scheme.*	pro ject, *to plan beforehand.*
prō test, *declaration.*	pro test, *to declare.*
rĕb el, *one that rebels.*	re bel, *to war against.*
rec ord, *note; register.*	re côrd, *to make record.*
ref use, *what is worthless.*	re fū̱se, *to deny; reject.*
rē print, *a second edition.*	re prĭnt, *to print again.*
re tail, *sale in small amounts.*	re tāil, *sell in small amounts.*

EXERCISE 271.

sŭb′ ject, *that under view.*	sub jĕct′, *to put under; subdue.*
suf fix, *what is suffixed.*	suf fix, *to fix after; to affix.*
sûr charge, *an excessive load.*	sur chärge, *to overload.*
sur name, *family name.*	sur nāme, *to give a surname.*
sur ve̤y, *view; measurement.*	sur ve̤y, *to view; to measure.*
sū pine, *sort of verbal noun.*	su pīne, *lying down; dull.*
tôr ment, *anguish.*	tor mĕnt, *to torture.*
trăj ect, *a passage over.*	tra ject, *throw over; cross.*
trans fer, *act of conveying.*	trans fĕr, *to convey; sell.*
trans port, *conveyance.*	trans pōrt, *convey as troops.*
un dress, *loose, negligent dress.*	un drĕss, *to take off clothes.*

EXERCISE 272.

coun′ ter-mănd, *a contrary order.*
coun ter-mănd′, *to revoke a command.*
in′ ter dĭct, *a prohibiting order; prohibition.*
in ter dĭct′, *to forbid by order; to prohibit.*
ō′ ver tûrn, *act of overturning; overthrow.*
o ver tûrn′, *to turn over; to overset; subvert.*
rĕp′ ri mănd, *rebuke; severe reproof.*
rep ri mănd′, *to rebuke; to reprove severely.*
at′ tri bute, *peculiar property; quality.*
at trĭb′ ute, *to impute; to assign; to ascribe to.*
mis con′ dŭct, *wrong conduct; ill-behavior.*
mis con dŭct′, *to conduct amiss; to mismanage.*

SECTION XII.

Words changed from nouns or adjectives, into verbs, by a change in pronunciation, in spelling, or in both.

EXERCISE 273.

clōse (*cloce*), *shut up; tight.*	cloṣe (*cloze*), *to shut up.*
grēase, *animal fat.*	grēaṣe, *to smear with fat.*
house, *place of residence.*	houṣe, *to shelter.*
mouse, *a rodent animal.*	mouṣe, *to catch mice.*
glȧss, *transparent substance.*	glāze, *to work with glass.*
brass, *alloy of copper and zinc.*	braze, *to solder with brass.*
grass, *herbage.*	graze, *to eat grass.*
ūse, *act of employing.*	ūṣe, *to employ.*
prīce, *value.*	prīze, *to set a value on.*
rise, *ascent; increase.*	riṣe, *to ascend; increase.*
life, *existence.*	lĭve, *to exist.*
wife, *a married woman.*	wīve, *to take for a wife.*
griēf, *sorrow.*	griēve, *to sorrow.*
prōōf, *test; evidence.*	prọve, *to test; to verify.*
thief, *one that steals.*	thiēve, *to steal.*

EXERCISE 274.

bäth, *a place to bathe in.* | bāthe, *to wash in a bath.*
brĕath, *air inhaled.* | brēathe, *to inhale air.*
clŏth, *fabric for garments.* | clōthe, *to furnish with clothes.*
lōath, *unwilling.* | lōathe, *to feel disgust for.*
wrēath, *garland; chaplet.* | wrēathe, *to twine or encircle.*
mouth, *aperture between the lips.* | mouth, *to speak affectedly.*
smōōth, *even; level.* | smōōth, *to make even.*

EXERCISE 275.

a būse′, *ill use.* | a būse′, *to use ill.*
mis use, *wrong use.* | mis use, *to use wrong.*
dif fuse, *copious.* | dif fuse, *to spread.*
ex cuse, *apology.* | ex cuse, *to apologize.*
ad vice, *counsel.* | ad vise, *to counsel.*
de vice, *design.* | de vise, *to design; to plan.*
be hōōf, *profit.* | be hōōve, *to become; befit.*
be liēf, *assent; faith.* | be liēve, *to assent to.*
re prōōf, *rebuke.* | re prove, *to rebuke; censure.*
prŏph′ e cy, *prediction.* | prŏph′ e sȳ, *to predict.*

Words *spelled alike*, but different in *pronunciation* and *meaning.*

EXERCISE 276.

bȧss, *a sea-fish; a tree.* | bāss, *deep; low; grave.*
bow, *to bend; act of reverence.* | bōw, *instrument to shoot arrows.*
dōve, *did dive.* | dȯve, *a pigeon.*
ġĭll, *fourth of a pint.* | gĭll, *breathing organ in fishes.*
gout, *disease of the small joints.* | gout (*goo*), *taste; relish.*
lēad, *to guide; conduct.* | lĕad, *soft, heavy metal.*
rēad, *to peruse.* | rĕad, *did read.*
lēase, *a contract.* | lēase, *to glean; gather.*

EXERCISE 277.

mow, *a pile of hay.* | mōw, *to cut down grass.*
row, *riot; tumult.* | rōw, *a range or series.*
slough, *a deep, miry place.* | slŭgh, *cast skin of a serpent.*
tēar, *fluid from the eyes.* | teâr, *to pull in pieces.*
wĭnd, *air in motion.* | wīnd, *to turn; twist.*
ĕn′ trance, *plan of entry.* | en trance′, *to put in a trance.*

SECTION XIII.

VARIABLE USAĠE.

This Section is designed to bring under view certain words and classes of words, in respect to which usage is variable, and which are not elsewhere specially noticed in this work.

EXERCISE 278.

vĭl′ lain	con nĕct′	in flĕct′
vil lain y *	con nec tion †	in flec tion
vil lain ies	con nex ion	in flex ion
vil lain ous	de flect	re flect
vil lain ous ly	de flec tion	re flec tion
vil lain ous ness	de flex ion	re flex ion

EXERCISE 279.

de fĕnse′ ‡	ex pĕnse′	of fĕnse′	prē tĕnse′
de fense less	ex pen sive	of fen sive	pre ten sion
de fen sive	ex pen sive ness	of fen sive ly	li′ cense
de fen so ry	ex pen sive ly	of fen sive ness	li cens er
de fen si ble	ex pense less	of fense less	li cens *ed*

EXERCISE 280.

wōe §	drou*gh*t ‖ (*drout*)	prăc′ tice ¶
wo′ ful	drought′ y	prac tiç *ed*
wo ful ly	drought i ness	prac tic ing
wo ful ness	hēi*gh*t ‖	prac tic er
woe-be-gōne	height *en*	prac ti cian

* These five are often improperly written without the *i*, as *villany*.

† The spelling with *t* is the preferable one in each of these cases.

‡ Written also with *c*, as *defence*, though never in the derivatives.

§ Often, though against analogy, written *wo* without the *e*, and, in the derivatives, almost always so.

‖ Very often written *drouth* and *hight* by the best authorities.

¶ As a *verb*, *practice* is mostly written with *s*, as *practise*. This difference between the noun and the verb is properly retained only where the final syllable is under the accent, as in *device*, *devise*. See Exercise 275.

EXERCISE 281.

tĕn′ a ble*	sŏlv′ a ble	ad mĭt′ ta ble
ten i ble	solv i ble	ad mit ti ble
ad da ble	ĭn′ fer a ble	rĕf′ er a ble
ad di ble	in fĕr′ ri ble	re fĕr′ ri ble
pärt a ble	con vẽrs a ble	trans fĕr a ble
part i ble	con vers i ble	trans fer ri ble

EXERCISE 282.

in clōṣe′†	in crŭst′	in gŭlf′	in rōll′
en cloṣe	en crust	en gulf	en roll
in cage	in gráft	in trust	in snáre
en cage	en graft	en trust	en snare
in case	in gôrge	in list	in sūre
en case	en gorge	en list	en sure
in trench	in grōss	in quīre	in thrall
en trench	en gross	en quire	en thrall
in dôrse	in fold	in trēat	in *w*răp
en dorse	en fold	en treat	en *w*rap

EXERCISE 283.

con fīde′, *entrust.*	de pĕnd′, *hang down from.*
cŏn′ fi dent,‡ *entrusting.*	de pend ent, *depending.*
con fi dant, *one entrusted.*	de pend ent, *a dependent.*
de scĕnd′, *come down.*	su per in tend′, *oversee.*
de scend ent, *descending.*	superintendent, *overseeing.*
de scend ant, *one descended.*	su per in tend ent, *overseer.*

* Of the adjectives, in English, ending in *able* or *ible*, by far the greater part end in *able*, while a few, as above, take either termination.

† The words in this Exercise take either form of the prefix (*in* or *en*) almost indifferently.

‡ In words of this class, it is usual to write the termination, *ent*, when the word is used as an *adjective*, and *ant*, when as a *noun*. But in the case of *dependent* and *superintendent*, usage seems well settled in favor of spelling the noun and the adjective both alike.

EXERCISE 284.

ā′ cre *	sā′ ber	mē′ ter	căl′ i ber
na cre	fi ber	mi ter	sep ul cher
lu cre	o cher	ni ter	wīṣe a cre
o gre	mau ger	cĕn ter	the a ter
ŏa gre	lŭs ter	spec ter	ac cou′ ter
li vre	om ber	e lĕc′ tre	con cĕn ter
ç hăn cre	am ber	salt pē ter	ren coun ter
măs′ sa cre	bis ter	ma neū ver	mē′ di ō cre

EXERCISE 285.

ad vīṣe′ †	dis guīṣe′,	sur prīṣe′
ap prise	pre mise	mis prise
de spise	sur mise	com prise
de vise	re vise	de mise
em prise	frăn′ chise	chas tise
ĕn′ ter prise	crit i cise	căt′ e chise
com pro mise	ad ver tise	cĭr cum cise
su per vīse′	ex er cise	dis frăn′ chise
af frăn′ chise	ex or cise	en fran chise

EXERCISE 286.

pŏl y hē′ dron ‡	ox′ īde ‡	mōld § }
pol y he dral	brō mīde	mōuld }
oc ta he dron	stē a rīne	mold er }
oc ta he dral	tan nin	mould er }
tet ra he dron	bī′ ped ‡	mold y }
tet ra he dral	quad ru ped	mould y }
pen ta he dron	cen ti ped }	mōlt }
pen ta he drons	cen ti pede }	mōult }

* Of this class of words, those in which the *er* is preceded by *c* or *g*, (with the exception of *mauger*), reverse the order of the letters and end in *re*, as *acre*, *lucre*, etc. The same is done in the words *livre* and *electre*.

† Some of the verbs in this Exercise are not unfrequently made to conform in spelling to the class of verbs ending in *ize*. The best usage, however, is in favor of writing them all as above.

‡ On *polyhedron*, see note, page 166; on *oxide*, *stearine*, etc., see note, page 168; on *biped*, *centiped*, etc., see note, page 163.

§ *Mould* and *moult*, with their derivatives, to be in analogy with such words as *bold*, *bolt*, etc., should be written, *mold*, *molt*, etc. The former, however, is the prevalent spelling.

SECTION XIV.

WORDS OF SIMILAR SIGNIFICATION.

One of the commonest errors in dealing with words of this class, in the school-room, is that of supposing them entirely *alike* in all their various meanings and applications. Hence, often, the highest advantage of the study, aside from the mere spelling, is all but lost; for the main point is to acquire the habit of *discriminating* between words that seem to be identical in meaning. With proper caution in this respect, few exercises will be found more interesting, as well as useful, than those presented in this Section.

EXERCISE 287.

quit	leave	dint	force	pate	head
arch	curve	scrub	scour	pawn	pledge
barge	boat	ford	wade	slag	dross
beak	bill	null	void	pest	plague
scowl	frown	sheen	bright	lurk	skulk
bāirn	child	râre	scârce	spite	spleen
purge	clĕanse	slake	quench	swab	mop
quäff	drink	sleek	smooth	vend	sell
fȧst	quick	aim	point	bare	mere
piērce	stab	liēge	lord	bear	yield

EXERCISE 288.

cite	quote	slink	sneak	clank	clang
quest	search	snack	shâre	clinch	clutch
quoth	say	speck	spot	corse	corpse
count	earl	cräunch	munch	heft	weight
blight	blȧst	gape	yawn	drill	bore
space	room	garb	dress	braid	weave
plait	fold	gloat	gaze	tĕrse	neat
tact	skill	gruff	grum	hoar	white
bid	call	blow	stroke	pitch	toss
bind	tie	rend	tear	grace	charm

EXERCISE 289.

fume	smoke	swāy	wiēld	twine	twist
barm	yēast	smash	breāk	booth	shed
lieū	stĕad	tramp	trĕad	date	time
heal	cure	dolt	dunce	queer	odd
jole	cheek	crowd	throng	quill	twill
marsh	mōōr	brĕadth	width	daub	smear
urge	press	bring	fetch	gorge	glut
bide	dwell	bilk	cheat	creep	crawl
delve	dig	blink	wink	kĭrk	church
noun	name	mate	match	moil	drudge
mire	mud	midge	*g*nat	mulct	fine

EXERCISE 290.

āye	yeā	yes	quĕrl	twīrl	whīrl
deem	think	judge	soak	steep	drench
dupe	gull	trick	ġin	snare	trap
lave	bathe	wạsh	rive	cleave	split
champ	chew	bite	dip	merge	plunge
speak	say	tell	bay	cove	gulf
bet	wage	stake	fuse	smelt	melt
web	weft	woof	guile	cráft	fraud
hist	hush	hark	väunt	boast	brag
troll	roll	bōwl	air	mien	look

EXERCISE 291.

brunt	shock	stroke	hunt	search	seek
scud	run	flee	wáft	float	swim
tweak	twinge	twitch	wince	shrink	flinch
wạnd	rod	stáff	bud	sprout	chit
aim	drift	scope	sneer	jeer	scoff
probe	test	try	skate	slide	glide
singe	scorch	parch	cope	strive	match
scath	harm	hurt	ạwe	dread	fear
reef	furl	fold	boor	lout	clown
heap	pile	máss	ask	beg	crave
flash	flare	gleam	gale	blast	gust

EXERCISE 292.

look	see	view	brink	edge	vērge
mash	smash	crush	sin	vice	crime
veer	turn	bend	bag	sack	pouch
crest	tuft	plume	raise	grow	rear
culm	stem	stạlk	bough	branch	limb
dart	lance	spear	bring	bear	fetch
froth	foam	spume	cute	keen	sharp
glee	fun	mirth	gape	gaze	stare
pile	heap	mass	pelt	hide	skin

EXERCISE 293.

coy	shy	blot	blur	spot	stain
jest	joke	bound	bounce	leap	spring
sort	kind	clan	race	tribe	horde
quit	leave	beach	shore	strand	coast
mole	mound	give	grȧnt	cede	yield
knar	knot	fling	cast	hurl	throw
tẽrm	word	flog	scoûrge	thrash	whip
win	gain	bray	pound	crush	brūiṣe
beast	brute	pace	step	gait	wạlk
broad	wide	dike	ditch	fosse	trench
flame	blaze	catch	sēize	grasp	snatch

EXERCISE 294.

sprig	twig	put	place	lay	set
store	shop	move	budge	stir	start
boss	knob	turf	sod	clod	glebe
scheme	plan	spare	gäunt	lank	lean
bloat	swell	globe	sphere	orb	ball
haste	speed	drag	draw	pull	haul
rock	stone	lift	heave	hoist	raise
whiff	puff	beat	baste	drub	pelt
wan	pale	pry	spy	peer	peep
tithe	tenth	stale	flat	dull	trite
twain	two	low	base	mean	vile

EXERCISE 295.

might	strength	reck	heed	mind	care
blow	stroke	chafe	rub	gall	fret
rasp	file	smite	strike	*k*nock	hit
grọwl	snarl	curl	crimp	crisp	crape
rent	lease	rōw	rank	line	file
shrub	bush	doze	drowse	nap	sleep
purge	clĕanse	fit	suit	fay	fadge
dint	force	bang	beat	thwack	thump
hunt	seek	screak	screech	scream	shriek
bleak	cold	*w*ring	*w*rest	*w*rench	twist

EXERCISE 296.

boon	gift	pres′ ent	tart	sour	aç′ id
blend	mix	miṉ gle	brush	broom	be ṣom
din	noise	clat ter	lees	dregs	ref use
graft	shoot	ci on	rẹin	curb	bri dle
ode	song	po em	frẹight	load	car go
blȧnch	bleach	whīt *e*n	haft	hilt	han dle
ire	*w*räth	aṉ ger	tome	book	vol ūme
quake	shake	shud der	sheath	case	scab bard
late	fresh	re cent	mute	dum*b*	si lent
fell	fierce	cru el	nude	bare	na ked

EXERCISE 297.

crave	long	haṉk′ er	track	trace	ves′ tige
spite	grudge	mal ice	newt	eft	liz ard
daṉk	moist	hu mid	work	toil	la bor
cleft	rent	fis sure	squab	dȯve	pig eon
blain	blotch	blis ter	spear	lȧnce	jav*e* lin
ledge	ridge	lay er	sōurce	spring	fount ain
right	claim	ti tle	pair	brace	coŭp le
stạll	crib	mān ger	cōlt	foal	fil ly
mix	blend	miṉ gle	box	chest	cof fer
muse	think	pon der	hide	mask	cȯv er
fight	war	bat tle	town	burgh	cit y

EXERCISE 298.

mild	meek	gen′ tle	brief	short	con cise′
quail	crouch	cow er	build	frame	con struct
fleet	swift	rap id	patch	mend	re pair
prompt	quick	rĕad y	creed	faith	be lief
stout	strong	stur dy	foil	thwart	de feat
duct	tube	chan nel	chat	ta*l*k	con vĕrse
gäunt	slim	slen der	fen	marsh	mo răss
clump	bunch	clus ter	seethe	boil	con coct
chink	crack	crev ice	hail	greet	sa lute
pine	droop	lan guish	guide	lead	con duct
free	frank	can did	stick	cling	ad here
serf	slave	bond man	big	large	bulk′ y
beau	fop	cox comb	cave	den	cav ern

EXERCISE 299.

spurn	scorn	dell	dale	vale	val′ ley
strōll	stray	pick	cull	sort	se lect′
weep	mourn	tress	curl	lock	ring′ let
crude	raw	sight	view	scene	pros pect
stănch	fĩrm	hear	hark	list	lis*t* en
pawn	pledge	feūd	fray	broil	quar rel
bluff	cliff	belt	sash	zone	gĩr dle
map	chart	clog	glut	gorge	sur feĭt
ruse	trick	dolt	mope	drone	slug gard

EXERCISE 300.

quaint	strange	tinge	tint	hue	cȯl′ or
hȧsp	clȧsp	mold	shape	form	fash ion
stint	tȧsk	rule	reign	sway	gȯv ern
cram	stuff	road	way	street	high way
crouch	cringe	taunt	scoff	mock	de ride′
glow	shine	ȧsk	beg	crave	im plore
sieve	screen	class	rank	grade	de gree
press	squeeze	have	hold	own	pos sess
prowl	rove	slack	loose	lax	re miss

EXERCISE 301.

fright	scare	chide	scold	blame	re buke′
neat	clean	vex	fret	tease	an noy
filth	dĭrt	cease	stop	quit	de sist
hoist	lift	act	deed	feat	ex ploit
stŏŏk	shock	blithe	gay	mer′ ry	spright′ly
goad	spur	frisk	skip	gam bol	frol ic
scowl	frown	mode	way	meth od	man ner
flay	skin	pack	load	bun dle	bur den
skip	dance	sing	chånt	car ol	war ble
limp	halt	spoil	prey	boot y	plun der
plod	drudge	roam	rove	ram ble	wạn der

EXERCISE 302.

hoot	shout	cave	grot	cav′ ern	grot′ to
nigh	near	wish	want	de ṣire′	cŏv et
pĕrk	prim	haste	speed	dis patch	hur ry
dike	trench	filch	steal	pur loin	pil fer
culm	stem	jade	tire	fa tïgue	wea ry
cråft	trade	tempt	lure	en tice	de coy′
cry	whine	aid	help	a bet	as sist
jäunt	trip	add	join	an nex	ad join
clump	chunk	beg	crave	be seech	im plore
hives	croup	loathe	hate	ab hor	de test
wile	trick	freak	whim	fan′ cy	ca prïce

EXERCISE 303.

fine	for′ feĭt	grace	mĕr′ cy	fa′ vor
chånce	fort une	hid	se cret	cŏv ert
cash	mŏn ey	brave	gal lant	val iant
shōal	shal low	harm	dam age	mis chĭef
dĕad	life less	fight	bat tle	com bat
choke	throt tle	smart	clev er	skill ful
choice	op tion	grief	sor row	sad ness
green	vĕr dant	fuss	tu mult	up roar
tọ̈ur	jour ney	post	pil lar	col um*n*
hawk	fạ̈*l* con	bent	curv *e*d	crook ed

EXERCISE 304.

wit	hu' mor	dirk	dag' ger	pon' iard
neigh	whin ny	dry	ar id	parch ed
plume	feath er	theme	sub ject	top ic
threat	men ace	trade	traf fic	com merce
bright	shīn ing	trice	mo ment	in stant
midst	mid dle	*w*reath	gar land	chap let
dearth	fam ine	zest	rel ish	fla vor
new	nov el	calm	plaç id	tran quil
shield	buck ler	old	a ged	se nīle
rage	fu ry	g*h*ost	spec ter	phan tom

EXERCISE 305.

frail	frag' ile	groove	fur' row	chan' nel
news	ti dings	hot	sul try	fer vid
sketch	out line	hide	cov er	shel ter
lim*b*	mem ber	lithe	pli ant	lim ber
part	por tion	fawn	flat' ter	whee' dle
maw	stom ach	too	al so	like wise
arms	weap ons	prop	ful crum	sup port'
thief	rob ber	fraught	fill *e*d	re plete
paint	pig ment	call	con voke'	sum' mon
clear	lu cid	rue	la ment	re gret'

EXERCISE 306.

mad	rab' id	choose	e lect'	se lect'
hard	sol id	daunt	ap pall	dis may
storm	tem pest	grant	ad mit	al low
test	tri al	mar	de face	im pair
style	dic tion	keep	re tain	pre serve
stream	cur rent	link	com bine	u nite
slight	neg lect'	shun	a void	es chew
strict	se vere	oust	e ject	ex pel
seem	ap pear	check	re strain	con trol
rest	re pose	niche	hol' low	re cess
use	em ploy	chase	fol low	pur sue
burst	ex plode	eke	length *e*n	pro long
build	con struct	foul	filth y	dirt' y

EXERCISE 307.

apt	fit	bad	wick'ed	e' vil	sin' ful
fib	lie	sly	cun ning	crȧft y	wi ly
fang	tusk	prate	prat tle	chat ter	bab ble
peat	turf	quick	ağ ĭle	act ive	nim ble
prong	tīne	head	chiēf tain	lead er	cap tain
kine	cows	drear	som ber	dis mal	gloom y
pool	pond	scribe	pen man	pen ner	wrīt er
cowl	hood	law	stat ute	e dict	de cree'
craw	crop	weak	sil ly	fool ish	ab surd

SECTION XV.

OPPOSITES.

In the study of words of this class, we learn by *contrast*, which is one of the most powerful modes of impressing thought. Everywhere in nature, we see *things* that are opposite—the *land*, the *sea*, the *lake*, the *island*, the *mountain*, the *valley*, *growth*, *decay*, etc. The attention of the pupil may be directed to this fact; so that, while studying the *words* that denote contrast, the distinctions may be more vividly impressed by considering the *things* which they indicate. This is often the best kind of *object teaching*.

EXERCISE 308.

love	hate	soft	hard	long	short
rich	poor	tame	wild	thick	thin
give	take	seek	shun	lost	found
first	last	meet	part	more	less
right	wrong	cool	warm	trụe	fạlse
roŭgh	smooth	back	front	fēast	fȧst
large	small	tight	loose	dark	light
don	doff	right	left	frown	smile
rise	fall	white	black	pēace	war
came	went	high	low	hĕad	foot

EXERCISE 309.

sink	swim	life	dĕath	strong	wēak
freeze	thaw	brēak	mend	cry	läugh
hill	dale	friĕnd	foe	fore	ȧft
day	night	dry	wet	push	pull
buy	sell	work	play	coax	drive
cold	hot	girl	boy	cheap	dear
sick	well	bride	groom	ebb	flōw
van	rear	bond	free	lad	lass
drake	duck	good	bad	sharp	dull
hope	fear	best	worst	height	depth

EXERCISE 310.

age	youth	east	west	joy	griēf
old	young	north	south	tọ	fro
king	queen	curse	bless	mild	fiērce
fresh	sạlt	bloom	fade	praise	blame
quick	slow	prow	stem	far	near
soon	late	teach	learn	grave	gay
buck	doe	fat	lean	save	waste
sparse	dense	lose	find	sweet	sour
bind	loose	fair	foul	cōarse	fine
gaunt	plum	front	back	sane	mad

EXERCISE 311.

want	plen' ty	straight	crook' ed
pale	rud dy	lēad	fol low
shame	*h*on or	hell	hĕav *e*n
wide	nar row	goose	gan der
lend	bor row	light	dark ness
kind	cru el	low	loft y
odd	e ven	pain	pleas ure
good	e vil	bold	mod est
truth	er ror	land	wạ ter
lake	ī*s* land	clear	cloud y
strait	ĭs*th* mus	niēce	neph ew

EXERCISE 312.

base	no′ ble	tough	ten′ der
joy	sor row	stiff	lim ber
vice	virt ue	wise	fool ish
slow	rap id	man	wom an
top	bot tom	clean	dirt y
late	ear ly	sweet	bit ter
full	emp ty	end	be gin′
deep	shal low	hope	de spair

EXERCISE 313.

a′ ged	yoūth′ ful	fēast′ ing	fȧst′ ing
care ful	care less	ab sence	pres̱ ence
for mer	lat ter	far ther	near er
doŭb le	sin gle	fear ful	fear less
buy er	sell er	curs ed	bless ed
broth er	sis ter	find er	lo̤s er
moth er	fä ther	i dle	bus y
up ward	down ward	a gue	fe ver

EXERCISE 314.

hith′ er	thith′ er	in′ let	out′ let
win ter	sum mer	in side	out side
need ful	need less	in ward	out ward
mid day	mid night	loos *en*	fȧs*t en*
land man	sēa man	ev er	nev er
no where	some where	dai ly	night ly
part ing	meet ing	of*t en*	sel dom
law yer	cli ent	peace ful	war like

EXERCISE 315.

sôme′ thing	nŏth′ ing	sun′ rise	sun′ set
stroŋ ger	weak er	tame ness	wild ness
gath er	scat ter	ad vȧnce′	re treat′
wake ful	sleep y	be fore	aft′ er
ab sent	pres ent	suc cess	fail ure
back ward	for ward	a bove	be low′
fore most	hind most	with in	with out

EXERCISE 316.

dĕb' it	crĕd' it	mā' jor	mī' nor
con vex	con cave	vĭc tor	vĭc tim
ab stract	con crete	van guard	rēar guard
lär board	stär board	jūn ior	sēn ior
lee ward	wind ward	môr tal	nā tal
friġ id	tor rid	păl lid	rŭd dy
pledġ er	pledġ ee'	zē nith	nā dir
cȯv ert	ō' vert	lănd lord	tĕn ant

EXERCISE 317.

in clude'	ex clude'	ex pand'	con tract'
con vĕrge	dĭ vĕrge	en th[illegible]e	de throne
re pel	pro pel	per s[illegible]	dis suade
ad vĕrt	a vĕrt	con se[illegible]	dis sent
ac cuse	ex cuse	en robe	dis robe
as cend	de scend	in hale	ex hale
at tach	de tach	in ject	[illegible] ject
in vest	di vest	in' gress	[illegible]' gress

SECTION XVI.

WORDS OF SIMILAR SIGNIFICATION.

EXERCISE 318.

hab' it	cus' tom	pil' lage	plun' der
ham let	vil lage	treat ment	ūs age
ha ven	har bor	dog ma	ten et
gēn ius	ta lent	thresh old	door-sill
ill ness	sick ness	ēa ger	ēar nest
mar riage	wed ding	pȧss port	li cense
ram part	bul wark	fam ish	pĕr ish
near ly	al most	tri graph	triph thong
wis dom	pru dence	noi some	nox ious
fĕr tile	fruit ful	mes sage	mis sion

EXERCISE 319.

cre' dence	cred' it	re fuse'	de cline'
scârce ly	hard ly	mis lēad	de lude
neū ter	nēi ther	be hest	com mánd
arc tic	north ern	per mit	al low
flee cy	wo͝ol ly	suc cum*b*	sub mit
lug gage	bag gage	re cant	re nounce
le vant	east ern	re ceive	ac cept
me ter	mĕas ure	in thrall	en slave
rig or	harsh ness	re pēal	re voke
rum mage	ran sack	re veal	di vulge
scar let	crim *s*on	in graft	in sert

EXERCISE 320.

co erce'	com pel'	re lax'	slack' *e*n
ac cost	ad dress	de sīgn	proj ect
con fess	a vow	re ply	an swer
ac quāint	in form	per plex	puz zle
con fute	re fute	an tïque	an cient
de vise	be queāth	ran' som	re deem'
con vince	per suade	ech o	re sound
dis burse	ex pend	ren der	re turn
de fend	pro tect	su*b*t le	a cute
de sire	re quest	al cove	re cess
con trive	in vent	no tice	re gard

EXERCISE 321.

glim' mer	glit' ter	ban' ner	en' sign	stand' ard
sole ly	mere ly	sil ly	sim ple	stu pid
bram ble	bri er	bau ble	gew gaw	tri fle
breāk er	bil low	pa gan	hēa then	gen tile
va cant	emp ty	shīn ing	brill iant	spark ling
box er	fīght er	ac rid	pun gent	bīt ing
mar tial	war like	as tral	stel lar	star ry
bod ice	cor set	ad der	ser pent	vi per
can ter	gal lop	bes tial	bēast ly	bru tish
be twixt'	be tween'	dam *s*el	maid *e*n	vir gin

EXERCISE 322.

cāi' tiff	vil' lain	budg' et	bun' dle	par' cel
er rand	mes sage	fa tal	mor tal	dĕad ly
col um*n*	pil lar	care ful	cau tious	watch ful
foi ble	fāil ing	gloss y	shīn y	lus trous
fra cas	up roar	mon ger	dēal er	trād er
func tion	of fice	re gal	roy al	prince ly
gus to	rel ish	toŭch y	tes ty	pet tish
im age	like ness	vi rus	ven om	poi son
vi ands	vict *u*als	suit or	woo er	lov er
wist ful	wish ful	er ror	blun der	mis take'
yearn ing	long ing	fic tion	nov el	ro mance

EXERCISE 323.

vent' ure	haz' ard	e' dict	fi' at	de cree'
war bler	song ster	awk ward	clum sy	un couth
ze ro	ci pher	coun sel	con sult'	ad vise
suc cor	re lieve'	mur mur	re pine	com plain
as sent'	con sent	car ry	con vey	trans port
con sīgn	com mit	to tal	en tire	com plete
de sire	re quest	al lure'	en tice	de coy
col late	com pâre	de port	de mēan	be have
a dieū	fare well	as sault	as sāil	at tack
pro tract	pro long	re veal	di vulge	dis close
im pede	ob struct	re fund	re pay	re store

EXERCISE 324.

max' im	ad' age	prov' erb	sāy' ing
fur bish	bur nish	pol ish	brīght *e*n
cus tom	du ty	im post	trib ute
loi ter	lin ger	säun ter	tăr ry
nurt ure	noŭr ish	cher ish	fos ter
in cense	o dor	per fume	fra grance
patch er	botch er	bun gler	cob bler
reck less	heed less	list less	care less
rāi ment	vest ure	vest ments	gar ments
gaud y	shōw y	taw dry	tin sel

EXERCISE 325.

cun′ ning	crȧft′ y	wi′ ly	art′ ful
se cret	hid den	la tent	oc cult′
cow ard	cra ven	das tard	pol troon
ho ly	sa cred	god ly	di vine
a base′	de grade′	dis grace′	hum′ ble
as pĕrse	tra duce	de fame	slȧn der
for give	ab solve	re mit	par don
pro vide	pro cure	sup ply	fur nish
de vour	en gorge	con sume	swal low
a droit	ex pert	dex′ trous	skill ful

EXERCISE 326.

al lege′	af fĭrm′	as sĕrt′	a vĕr′
ac quire	at tāin	ob tain	pro cure
ex ceed	ex cel	sur pȧss	out dọ
be wāil	be mōan	la ment	de plore
in fest	an noy	dis turb	mo lest
ar range	dis pose	di rect	di gest
com prise	em brace	con tāin	in clude
ac cuse	ar rāign	im pēach	cen′ sure
re spect	re gard	es teem	*h*on or
af flict	dis tress	troŭb′ le	har ass

EXERCISE 327.

vig′ or	en′ er gy	sti′ pend	sal′ a ry
fer vor	ar den cy	mis chief	in ju ry
pil grim	trav el er	vi brate	os cil late
port ly	cor pu lent	en ter	pen e trate
ti tle	ep i thet	viṣ age	coun te nance
sched ule	cat a logue	ban quet	fes ti val
prox y	sub sti tute	pul sate	pal pi tate
sur plus	o ver plus	que rist	ques tion er
lan guor	las si tude	watch ful	vig i lant
wor thy	laud a ble	spe cious	plaus i ble
flu ent	vol u ble	vic tor	con *q*u*er or
ri val	em u late	band age	lig a ture

EXERCISE 328.

sen′ try	sen′ ti nel	rapt′ ure	ec′ sta sy
hope less	des pe rate	pow er	fac ul ty
sav age	bar ba rous	an guish	ag o ny
post ure	at ti tude	oft times	fre quent ly
coŭr age	for ti tude	oint ment	lin i ment
gar nish	dec o rate	per il	jĕop ar dy
sanc tion	rat i fy	car riage	ve hĭ cle
new ness	nov el ty	pet tish	pet u lent

EXERCISE 329.

gar′ ner	grăn′ a ry	hom′ age	fe′ al ty
fe brīle	fe ver ish	mid riff	di a phragm
bane ful	poi son ous	bo nus	pre mi um
bound less	lim it less	con quest	vic to ry
con vent	nun ner y	con cord	har mo ny
sor did	nig gard lȳ	sup ple	pli a ble
glēan ing	gath er ing	house hold	fam i ly
låst ly	fi nal ly	lithe ness	lim ber ness

EXERCISE 330.

fore′ taste	an′ te past	a chiēve′	ac com′ plish
liv ing	live li hood	of fense	dis plĕas ure
in come	rev e nue	se clude	se ques ter
be hoof′	ad van′ tage	fore go	re lin quish
de tect	dis cov er	cha′ os	con fu sion
do main	do min ion	ver sion	trans la tion
re main	con tin ue	fisc al	fi nan cial
en chant	en rapt ure	ex tant	ex ist ing

EXERCISE 331.

guīd′ ance	di rec′ tion	haugh′ ty	dis dain′ ful
her ald	pro claim er	lus cious	de lĭ cious
down cåst	de ject ed	cloth ing	ap păr el
chair man	pres′ i dent	res cue	de liv er
li cense	per mis′ sion	let ter	e pis tle
mon strous	pro dig ious	swin dler	de fraud er
man date	in junc tion	con tract	in dent ure
doc tor	phy sĭ cian	sem blance	re sem blance

EXERCISE 332.

an nul′	nul′ li fy	re fine′	pu′ ri fy
di gress	de vi ate	re vile	vil i fy
en rich	fer til ize	in struct	ed i fy
e vince	man i fest	in cite	in sti gate
re miss	neg li gent	e vent	in ci dent
be quest	leg a cy	de void	des ti tute
re tort	rep ar tee′	per sist	per se vere′
gain′ say	con tra dict	van′ ish	dis ap pear

EXERCISE 333.

gris′ tle	car′ ti lage	mon′ strous	e nôr′ mous
hear er	ạu di tor	rats bane	ar′ se nic
luck y	fort u nate	full ness	plen i tude
night mare	in cu bus	hiss ing	sib i lant
cau tion	wa ri ness	few ness	pau ci ty
hate ful	o di ous	thun der	ful mi nate
ha tred	o di um	war rior	cham pi on
sur name	cog nō′ men	all spice	pi men′ to

EXERCISE 334.

peace′ ful	hal′ cy on	in fĭrm′	de crep′ it
spit tle	sa li′ va	be numb	stu′ pe fy
warn ing	mo nĭ tion	as sume	ar ro gate
fick le	ca prĭ cious	ar rest	ap pre hend′
black lead	plum ba go	dis turb	dis com pose
leap year	bis sex tile	for bid	in ter dict
de cide′	de ter mine	con cur	co in cide
con test	lit′ i gate	neg lect	dis re gard

EXERCISE 335.

bash′ ful	mod′ est	dif′ fi dent
for tress	cas *t*le	cit a del
am ple	spa cious	ca pa′ cious
al ien	strān ger	for′ eĭ*g*n er
fault less	blame less	in no cent
ān gel	spir it	mes sen ger
stub born	will ful	ob sti nate
bäl*m* y	fra grant	o dor ous

EXERCISE 336.

bra̤wn′ y	flesh′ y	mus′ cu lar
ram part	breast work	par a pet
bright ness	splen dor	brill ian cy
co gent	ur gent	fōr ci ble
con vict	cul prit	crim i nal
wa̤n ness	pale ness	pal lid ness
mi ser	nig gard	cur mud′ geon
tur ret	tow e̤r	min′ a ret

EXERCISE 337.

pa̤u′ per	beg′ gar	men′ di cant
sa ber	fa̤l chion	cim e ter
fun ny	com ic	läugh a ble
tac it	si lent	taç i turn
sam ple	pat tern	speç i men
a pex	sum mit	pin na cle
pa̤l try	pet ty	triv i al
jus tice	just ness	eq ui ty

EXERCISE 338.

cȯm′ rade	fel′ low	com pan′ ion
tri al	ef fort	en dĕav or
ty ro	nȯv ice	be gin ner
ad vent	com ing	ar ri val
con flict	strug gle	ren coun ter
ref uge	shel ter	a sy lum
se riēs	se quence	suc ces sion
vap id	taste less	in sip id

EXERCISE 339.

vēr′ dict	judg′ ment	de cis′ ion
bane ful	bale ful	per nĭ cious
wait er	sērv ant	do mes tic
cease less	end less	e tēr nal
clo ven	part ed	di vīd ed
scan dal	dis grace′	dis cred it
con cēal′	dis guise	dis sem ble
con cēive	sup pose	im aġ ine

EXERCISE 340.

con sīgn′	trans fĕr′	de liv′ er
dis mȧsk	un mȧsk	un cȯv er
a muse	di vĕrt	en ter tāin′
dis claim	re nounce	dis a vow
be long	per tain	ap per tāin
cap size	up set	o ver tûrn
con′ quer	van′ quish	o ver cȯme
bull y	hec tor	dom i neer

EXERCISE 341.

till′ age	farm′ ing	cult′ ure	hus′ band ry
hand some	pret ty	come ly	beau ti ful
ac tion	post ure	gest ure	at ti tude
fab ric	buīld ing	struct ure	ed i fice
glu ey	stick y	vis cous	glu ti nous
duc tile	flex ile	lim ber	flex i ble
rōam er	ram bler	strōll er	wan der er
run let	brook let	strēam let	riv u let

EXERCISE 342.

pee′ vish	fret′ ful	spleen′ y	splen′ e tic
plot ter	plan ner	schēm er	con trīv′ er
ra tion	por tion	pit tance	al low ance
pu pil	lĕarn er	schol ar	dis ci ple
o men	pre sage	to ken	prog nos tic
state ly	pomp ous	au gust′	ma jes tic
re bus	rid dle	ça rade	e nig ma
chas ten	pun ish	chas tise	cas′ ti gate

EXERCISE 343.

lav′ ish	waste′ ful	pro fuse′	prod′ i gal
ban ter	ral ly	de ride	rid i cule
hu mor	fan cy	ca prïce	va ga′ ry
suf fer	al low′	per mit	tol′ er ate
a non′	a pace	quick′ ly	speed i ly
ful fill	com plete	per form′	ex e cute
en roll	en list	re cord	reġ is ter
mis chȧnce	mis hap	ill-luck	mis fort′ une

EXERCISE 344.

aug ment′	en large′	ex tend′	am′ pli fy
a maze	con found	as tound	as ton′ ish
as cribe	im pute	as sīgn	at trib ute
be troth	af fy	es pouse	af fi ance
a rouse	ex cite	be stīr	a wāk en
con′ strue	ex plain	ex pound	in tēr pret
a bate′	less′ en	de crease	di min ish
tran′ quil	qui et	pēace′ ful	peace′ a ble

EXERCISE 345.

child′ ish	youth′ ful	pu′ er ile	ju′ ve nile
car nage	slaugh ter	butch er y	mas sa cre
won der	mar vel	mir a cle	prod i gy
sun dry	di vers	va ri ous	sev er al
thrall dom	bond age	slāv er y	sērv i tude
off spring	chil dren	prog e ny	de scend′ ants
bal ance	rem nant	reş i due	re māin der
plēad er	law yer	ad vo cate	de fend er

EXERCISE 346.

for′ mer	pri′ or	pre′ vi ous	pre cēd′ ing
scoff er	mock er	de lūd′ er	de rīd er
mind ful	heed ful	at ten tive	ob serv ant
dâr ing	däunt less	cou ra geous	de fi ant
tu tor	teach er	pre cep tor	in struct or
pur suit′	call ing	vo ca tion	em ploy ment
an nul	re pēal′	a bol ish	ab′ ro gate
en trēat	be seech	so liç it	sup pli cate

EXERCISE 347.

ex cuse′	de fend′	ex cul′ pate	jus′ ti fy
de note	im ply	in′ di cate	sig ni fȳ
in duce	im pel	act u ate	in flu ence
for sake	de şert	a ban′ don	re lin′ quish
sērv′ ice	a vail	ben′ e fit	ad van tage
her mit	re cluse	anch o ret	as cet ic
wor ship	a dore	ven er ate	rev′ er ence
a vērse′	back′ ward	un will′ ing	re luc′ tant

EXERCISE 348.

con dīgn′	wȯr′ thy	de sērv′ ed	mer′ it ed
fi nesse	çhï cane′	art′ i fice	strat a gem
ruth′ less	pit′ i less	du ra ble	pēr ma nent
dwell er	a bīd′ er	reş i dent	so′ journ er
pro voke′	tan′ ta lize	ir ri tate	ag gra vate
be witch	cap ti vate	fas ci nate	en am′ or
dis′ cord	dis sen′ sion	con ten′ tion	va′ ri ance
tempt er	en tiç er	al lūr er	se dū′ cer

EXERCISE 349.

tim′ id	tim′ or ous	cow′ ard ly
mad man	lu na tic	ma ni ac
clem ent	le ni ent	mer ci ful
doç ile	teach a ble	tract a ble
tru ly	ver i ly	re al ly
deft ly	skill ful ly	dex trous ly
hal low	con se crate	ded i cate
wa ver	fluc tu ate	vaç il late

EXERCISE 350.

tire′ some	te′ di ous	wēa′ ri some
wĕalth y	op u lent	af flu ent
wȯn drous	won der ful	mar vel ous
fawn er	syc o phant	par a site
speak er	or a tor	de claim′ er
de cent	dec o rous	be cȯm ing
cost ly	sump tu ous	ex pen sive
ex it	ex o dus	de part ure

EXERCISE 351.

har′ dy	res′ o lute	in trep′ id
con trite	pen i tent	re pent ant
*k*nāv ish	fraud u lent	dis *h*on est
wiz ard	cȯn jur er	en chȧnt er
whōl ly	to tal ly	com plete ly
mod el	par a di*g*m	ex am ple
ad verse	re pug′ nant	con flict ing
rest ing	re pōs ing	qui es cent

EXERCISE 352.

fruit′ ful	pro lif′ ic	pro duc′ tive
cas cade′	wa′ ter fall	cat′ a ract
con tent	sat is fy	grat i fy
mis rule	an arch y	dis or′ der
es trange	al ien ate	dis af fect′
re prove	rep ri mand	rep re hend
slack′ ness	re miss′ ness	neg′ li gence
fa tïgue′	wea′ ri ness	las si tude

EXERCISE 353.

dom′ i cil	res′ i dence	pẽr′ ma nent	du′ ra ble
a que ous	wa ter y	con di ment	sēa son ing
el e ment	ru di ment	mod i fy	qual i fy
cẽr ti fy	tes ti fy	per fi dy	trĕach er y
dep u ty	del e gate	tem per ate	mod er ate
des pot ism	tyr an ny	vaç il late	fluc tu ate
cor ri dor	gal ler y	sanc ti ty	ho li ness
po ta ble	drink a ble	meth od ize	sys tem ize

EXERCISE 354.

hor′ ri ble	ter′ ri ble	in′ su late	is′ o late
im mo late	sac ri fice	in fa mous	scan dal ous
grav i ty	so ber ness	leġ i ble	rēad a ble
äl ma nac	cal en dar	sol i tude	lone li ness
ar du ous	dif fi cult	se cre cy	pri va cy
ru mi nate	med i tate	ran cor ous	vĭr u lent
in ter im	in ter val	nu di ty	na ked ness
wise a cre	sim ple ton	plĕas ant ry	mer ri ment

EXERCISE 355.

stim′ u late	en cour′ age	con′ fi dence	re li′ ance
ad e quate	suf fĭ cient	dis so nant	dis cord ant
du bi ous	un cer tain	mal a dy	dis tem per
ban ish ment	ex pul sion	pec u late	em bez zle
am a zon	vi ra go	gar ru lous	lo qua cious
cher u bic	an gel ic	an i mate	en lĭv en
con ver sant	fa mil iar	coun sel or	ad viş er
cor por ate	col lec tive	o ver ture	pro pōs al

EXERCISE 356.

mock′ er y	de ris′ ion	con trĭ′ tion	pen′ i tence
ŏn er ous	bûr′ den some	ec stat ic	rap tur ous
por ti co	pi az′ za	ex am ine	scru ti nize
a pos′ tate	ren′ e gade	fa ce tious	hu mor ous
pū is sant	pow er ful	pa tēr nal	fa ther ly
ca thar tic	purg a tive	ma ter nal	mŏth er ly
ce les tial	hĕav en ly	fra ter nal	broth er ly
con sōl er	cŏm fort er	e lix ir	cor di al

EXERCISE 357.

ath let′ ic	vig′ or ous	au then′ tic	gen′ u ine
re sem ble	im i tate	o pin ion	sen ti ment
mo men tum	im pe tus	a bate ment	de duc′ tion
pre dic tion	proph e cy	ap por tion	dis trib ute
mo rose ness	sul len ness	at trac tive	al lūr ing
al lu sion	ref er ence	e lu sive	e va sive
dis sem bler	hyp o crite	con trīv ance	in ven tion
re hēars al	re cīt′ al	con clu sive	de ci sive

EXERCISE 358.

fru ĭ′ tion	en joy′ ment	in vent′ or	con triv′ er
ces sa tion	sus pen sion	im pel lent	im pul sive
con junc tion	con nec tion	pro tect ive	de fen sive
co er cion	com pul sion	tu ĭ tion	in struc tion
er rat ic	ec cen tric	pe ti tion	en trēat y
ex ac tion	ex tor tion	con du cive	pro mo tive
ex cep tion	ex clu sion	ġi gan tic	e nor mous
for bid ding	re pul sive	de lūd er	de cēiv er

EXERCISE 359.

col lec′ tion	as sem′ blage	in′ tri cate	com′ pli cate
se clu sion	re tire ment	vo ta ry	dev o tee′
ac ces sion	ad dĭ tion	me di ate	in ter cede
re cum bent	re clīn ing	gas con ade′	bra va′ do
il le gal	un law ful	in dis pose	dis in cline′
in ces sant	un cēas ing	dis a buse	un de ceive
in tes tine	in ter nal	dis al low	dis ap prove
rec ol lect′	re mem ber	fas′ ci nate	cap′ ti vate

EXERCISE 360.

in′ do lence	i′ dle ness	la′ zi ness
fẽr vent ly	ar dent ly	zĕal ous ly
per ti nent	ap po site	sūit a ble
priv i ly	pri vate ly	se cret ly
ed i ble	es cu lent	eat a ble
bash ful ness	mod est y	dif fi dence
ar a ble	plow a ble	till a ble
spright li ness	viv id ness	live li ness

EXERCISE 361.

or′ i fice	ap′ er ture	o′ pen ing
fu gi tive	run a gate	run a way
clar i fy	def e cate	pu ri fy
quer u lous	mur mur ing	com plain′ ing
rav *e*n ing	rav *e*n ous	ra pa cious
bur i al	sep ul ture	in ter ment
can di date	ap pli cant	as pīr ant
sub sẽ quent	fol low ing	suc ceed ing

EXERCISE 362.

cod′ i cil	sup′ ple ment	ap pen′ dix
ạu thor ize	em pow′ er	com mis sion
ca ter er	pur vẹy or	pro vīd er
com ic al	di vert ing	a mūs ing
jĕop ard ize	im per il	en dān ger
dis pir′ it	dis heärt *e*n	dis coŭr age
de file ment	pol lu tion	cor rup tion
ac cum bent	re cum bent	re clīn ing

EXERCISE 363.

en com′ pass	en cīr′ cle	en vi′ ron
spec ta tor	ob sẽrv er	be hold er
dif fu sion	dis per sion	ex ten sion
de mean or	de pōrt ment	be hāv ior
al lure ment	en tice ment	temp ta tion
u ten sil	im′ ple ment	in′ stru ment
em phat ic	im press′ ive	for ci ble
in ter dict′	in hib it	pro hib′ it

EXERCISE 364.

per′ il ous	haz′ ard ous	dān′ ger ous
som no lence	drow si ness	sleep i ness
al i ment	nu tri ment	nour ish ment
com plāi sant	af fa ble	court e ous
co pi ous	plen ti ful	a bun′ dant
way ward ness	fro ward ness	per vĕrse ness
nu tri tive	nu trĭ′ tious	noûr′ ish ing
crab bed ness	crust′ i ness	sûr li ness
ar gu er	rēa son er	de bāt′ er
om in ous	por tent′ ous	fore bōd ing
pre dict′ or	pre sāġ er	fore tell er

EXERCISE 365.

tent	tab′ er na cle	steep	pre cip′ i tous
just	eq ui ta ble	flay	ex co ri ate
frith	es tu a ry	scare	in tim i date
spy	em is sa ry	guide	di rect o ry
verge	ex trem′ i ty	fond	af fec tion ate
zeal	en thu si asm	awe	ven e ra′ tion
*h*eir	in her it or	fame	rep u ta tion
birth	na tiv i ty	praise	com men da tion
depth	pro fun di ty	flaw	im per fec tion
same	i den tic al	flash	cor us ca tion
rash	pre cip i tate	search	ex plo ra tion
speed	ve loç i ty	sport	rĕc re a tion

EXERCISE 366.

love′ ly	a′ mi a ble	stand′ ard	cri te′ ri on
tar dy	dil a to ry	frail ty	in firm i ty
friend ly	am i ca ble	li my	cal ca re ous
styl ish	fash ion a ble	west ern	hes pe ri an
ve nal	mer ce na ry	anx ious	so lic it ous
time ly	sea son a ble	a dapt	ac com mo date
rōv ing	mi gra to ry	zĕal ot	en thu si ast
mid dling	me di o cre	moist ure	hu mid i ty
ripe ness	ma tu′ ri ty	same ness	i den ti ty
swift ness	ra pid i ty	life less	in an i mate

EXERCISE 367

cur′ dle	co ag′ u late	dwell′ er	in hab′ it ant
toil some	la bo ri ous	rash ness	te mer i ty
art ist	ar tif′ i cer	be hĕad′	de cap i tate
pen sion	an nu i ty	con dense	con sol i date
spe cial	par tic u lar	at tend	ac com pa ny
en voy	em bas sa dor	ex cuse	a pol o gy
name less	a non y mous	de stroy	an ni hi late
pre vail′	pre dom i nate	dis sect	a nat o mize
a dopt	af fil i ate	blood y	san′ gui na ry
en rage	ex as pe rate	par take	par tiç′ i pate
de test	a bom i nate	boast′ fụl	os ten ta′ tious
dis card	re pu di ate	com ment	ex pla na tion
un like	dis sim i lar	priest ly	saç er do tal
e clipse	ob scu ra′ tion	learn ing	er u dĭ tion

EXERCISE 368.

main′ ly	chief′ ly	prin′ ci pal ly
hein ous	fla grant	ag gra va ted
no ted	mark *e*d	cel e bra ted
gor mand	glut t*o*n	gor mand iz er
dis trict	re gion	ter ri to ry
bliss ful	hap py	fe lic′ it ous
le gal	law ful	le git i mate
ord nance	can non	ar til ler y
health ful	*w*hole some	sa lu bri ous

EXERCISE 369.

a bridge′	short′ *e*n	ab bre′ vi ate
ad vice	coun sel	ad mo ni′ tion
ab surd	fool ish	pre pos ter ous
prob′ lem	ques tion	prop o si′ tion
clam or	out cry	ex cla ma tion
āb solve′	re lease′	ex on′ er ate
de pict	por tray	de lin e ate
fear′ ful	a fraid	ap pre hen′ sive
bet ter	im prove	a mēl′ io rate

EXERCISE 370.

dry′ ness	ar′ id ness	a rid′ i ty
dou*b*t ful	du bi ous	am big u ous
mos lem	mus sul man	Mo ham med an
squeam ish	scru pu lous	fas tid i ous
wa̤n ton	lech er ous	las civ i ous
press ing	stren u ous	im por tu nate
stal wart	vig or ous	re dou*b*t a ble
base ness	tur pi tude	de prav i ty
pray er	or i s̤on	sup pli ca′ tion
witch craft	sor cer y	con ju ra tion
shrewd ness	a cute′ ness	pen e tra tion

EXERCISE 371.

a bode′	res′ i dence	hab i ta′ tion
re proach	ob lo quy	op pro′ bri um
prog ress	im prove′ ment	pro fi cien cy
hos tile	un friend ly	in im ic al
pon der	con sid er	de lib er ate
prop er	pe cūl iar	ap pro pri ate
tri umph	o va tion	ex ul ta′ tion
mag ic	en chȧnt ment	in can ta tion
change a ble	mu′ ta ble	va′ ri a ble
trai tor ous	treach er ous	in sid′ i ous
rel e vant	per ti nent	ap′ pli ca ble

EXERCISE 372.

te′ di um	irk′ some ness	wea′ ri some ness
pil la ging	plun der ing	pred a to ry
sport ive ness	play ful ness	hi lăr′ i ty
dy nas ty	gov ern ment	sȯv′ er e̤*ig*n ty
vi o lent	fu ri ous	im pet′ u ous
faith ful ness	trust i ness	fi del i ty
prob i ty	*h*on es ty	in teg ri ty
bois ter ous	tur bu lent	tu mult u ous
serv i tude	slāv ish ness	ser vil i ty
du te ous	du ti ful	o be di ent
sa ving ness	thrift i ness	fru gal i ty

EXERCISE 373.

cor′ pu lence	flesh′ i ness	o bes′ i ty
*k*nāv ish ness	*k*nāv er y	dis hon es ty
laud a ble	praise wor thy	com mend a ble
op po site	con tra ry	an ti thet′ ic
an ces tor	fore fa ther	pro gen′ i tor
hand i craft	work man ship	man u fact′ ure
col lo quy	di a logue	con ver sa tion
dens i ty	com pact′ ness	so lid′ i ty
quạn da ry	di lem ma	per plex i ty
de cen cy	de co rum	pro pri e ty
con tra band	for bid den	pro hib it ed

EXERCISE 374.

em′ bas sy	le ga′ tion	dep u ta′ tion
des o late	de sert ed	sol′ i ta ry
a bet′ tor	fo ment er	in sti ga tor
pro pi tious	aus pi cious	fa vor a ble
re lent less	re morse less	un pit′ y ing
com ple tion	ful fill ment	ac com plish ment
ex pert ness	a droit ness	dex ter i ty
ad ja cent	ad join ing	con tig u ous
as ser tion	a ver ment	dec la ra′ tion
ap prāiṣ al	ap prize ment	val u a tion
se di tion	re bell ion	in sur rec tion

EXERCISE 375.

ab hor′ rence	a ver′ sion	dĕt es ta′ tion
in frac tion	in fringe ment	vi o la tion
ad journ ment	post pone ment	pro ro ga tion
de struc tion	sub ver sion	dem o li tion
im pēach ment	in dīct ment	ac cu sa tion
ac quire ment	at tain ment	ac qui si tion
ad ven ture	en′ ter prise	un der tak ing
ad just ment	set tle ment	reg u la tion
a dorn ment	or na ment	em bel′ lish ment
pri mĕ val	prim i tive	o rig in al
ma gi cian	sor cer er	nec′ ro man cer

SECTION XVII.

PARONYMOUS WORDS.

BY paronymous words are here meant such as are alike in *pronunciation*, but different in *spelling* and *meaning*.

The words of this class, it will be noticed, are here arranged according to the *vowel element* in each, however represented.*

EXERCISE 376.

ā

Bāle, *pack of goods.*
Bail, *surety.*
Ale, *malt liquor.*
Ail, *to trouble; distress.*
Sale, *act of selling.*
Sail, *to move by sails.*
Hale, *sound; healthy.*
Hail, *frozen drops of rain.*
Male, *a he-animal.*
Mail, *letter-bag.*
Fāne, *temple, or shrine.*
Fain, *gladly; willingly.*
Fe̱ign, *pretend.*

ā

Pāle, *wan; whitish.*
Pail, *open vessel for water, etc.*
Tale, *a story.*
Tail, *the end.*
Vale, *a valley.*
Vail, *covering for the face.*
Wale, *ridge; mark with wales.*
Wail, *lament; bemoan.*
Lane, *narrow way, or road.*
Lain, *extended; being at rest.*
Vāne, *weathercock.*
Vain, *conceited.*
Vein, *blood-vessel.*

* For example, the *regular long sound* of *a* is represented in six or seven different ways; for *a* in *ale*, *ai* in *mail*, *ei* in *vein*, *ea* in *break*, *e* in *fete*, *au* in *gauge*, *ey* in *prey*, *ay* in *bays*, are all exactly alike in *sound*, though different in *form* from each other. In words of more than one syllable, it should be added, the point of identity, on which the arrangement is based, lies in the *accented* syllable.

The words in this Section, and in the next, offer numerous illustrations of the powers and uses of the vowels, *Regular*, *Occasional*, and *Exceptional*, and should be studied in this view particularly.

EXERCISE 377.

ā

Māne, *hair on the neck of a beast.*
Main, *chief; the ocean.*
Pane, *a square of glass.*
Pain, *distress.*
Plane, *to make smooth.*
Plain, *level; clear.*
Ate, *did eat.*
Ait, *little island.*
Eight, *twice four.*
Bate, *to abate; deduct from.*
Bait, *a lure; to harass.*

ā

Rāin, *water from the clouds.*
Rẹin, *strap of a bridle.*
Rẹign, *to rule, as a king.*
Wane, *decrease.*
Wain, *a wagon.*
Base, *vile; mean.*
Bass, *gravest part of music.*
Brake, *tool for dressing flax.*
Break, *to sever by force.*
Chaste, *pure; undefiled.*
Chased, *pursued.*

EXERCISE 378.

ā

Fāte, *lot; destiny.*
Fẹte, *a feast.*
Gate, *door, or entrance.*
Gait, *mode of walking.*
Grate, *range of bars; to rub.*
Great, *large; vast.*
Nave, *hub of a wheel.*
Knave, *a cheat.*
Place, *situation.*
Plaice, *a flat-fish.*

ā

Phrāse, *expression.*
Fraise, *defense of pointed stakes.*
Frays, *broils; combats.*
Gage, *to pledge.*
Gauge, *a measure.*
Maze, *intricacy.*
Maize, *Indian corn.*
Wade, *to ford.*
Wẹighed, *did weigh.*
Waste, *spend lavishly.*
Waist, *middle of the body.*

EXERCISE 379.

ā

Plāte, *flat piece of metal.*
Plait, *to fold.*
Raze, *to subvert; demolish.*
Raise, *to lift up.*
Stake, *a post; a wager.*
Steak, *slice of meat.*
Bay, *gulf; a color.*
Bẹy, *a Turkish governor.*

ā

Wāit, *stay; delay.*
Wẹight, *heaviness.*
Wave, *a billow.*
Waive, *give up; put off.*
Faint, *weak; languid.*
Fẹint, *false show; pretense.*
Braze, *to solder with brass.*
Brays, *does bray.*

EXERCISE 380.

ā

Bāize, *coarse woolen cloth.*
Bays, *laurels.*

Dāy, *time from sunrise to sunset.*
Dey, *governor of Algiers.*

Slay, *kill.*
Sley, *a weaver's reed.*
Sleigh, *carriage on runners.*

Way, *road, or path.*
Weigh, *to balance; poise.*

Nay, *no.*
Neigh, *to whinny, as a horse.*

ā

Hāy, *dried grass.*
Hey, *an expression of joy.*
Prāy, *entreat; supplicate.*
Prey, *spoil; booty.*
Strait, *close; narrow path.*
Straight, *direct.*
Tray, *small trough; a waiter.*
Trey, *the three at cards or dice.*
Braid, *to weave; twisted cord.*
Brayed, *did bray, as an ass.*
Paste, *dough for pies; sticky substance.*
Paçed, *did pace.*

EXERCISE 381.

ā

Bāt' ing, *abating; excepting.*
Bait ing, *putting on bait.*

Grat er, *instrument to grate with.*
Great er, *larger.*

Raz ing, *overthrowing; destroying.*
Rais ing, *lifting; exalting.*

Strait en, *to narrow; stint.*
Straight en, *to make straight.*

Strait ly, *narrowly.*
Straight ly, *in a straight line.*

ā

A vāle, *to let down; depress.*
A vail, *to profit.*
Cham pagne, *a kind of wine.*
Cham paign, *level country.*
In vade, *to assail; attack.*
In veigh ed, *did inveigh.*
Ce ta' ceous, *having the nature of whales.*
Se ta ceous, *having the nature of bristles.*
Sal' a ble, *that may be sold.*
Sail a ble, *that may be sailed over.*

EXERCISE 382.

ē

Bē, *to exist.*
Bee, *an insect.*
Cede, *to yield; give up.*
Seed, *to sow, or scatter seed.*
Cere, *to cover with wax.*
Sear, *to burn; dry; withered.*
Seer, *a prophet.*

ē

Mēte, *to measure.*
Meet, *to assemble; suitable.*
Meat, *flesh for food.*

Scene, *a view, or sight.*
Seen, *beheld.*
Seine, *large fishing net.*

EXERCISE 383.

ē

Hēre, *in this place.*
Hear, *to perceive by the ear.*
Beer, *a malt liquor.* [*dead.*
Bier, *hand carriage for the*
Beet, *a garden vegetable.*
Beat, *to strike ; throb.*
Breech, *lower part of the body.*
Breach, *a break ; a gap.*
Ceil, *overlay the top of a room.*
Seal, *marine animal ; stamp.*
Creek, *small stream, or inlet.*
Creak, *a harsh, grating sound.*

ē

Thē, *definite article.*
Thee, *thyself.*
Beech, *name of a tree.*
Beach, *the sea-shore.*
Cheep, *to chirp, as a bird.*
Cheap, *low-priced.*
Deer, *a wild animal.*
Dear, *beloved ; costly.*
Feet, *plural of foot.*
Feat, *exploit ; deed.*
Fees, *rewards.* [*a rope.*
Feaze, *to untwist, as the end of*

EXERCISE 384.

ē

Freeze, *to congeal.*
Frieze, *coarse cloth ; a cornice.*
Greece, *name of a country.*
Grease, *fat.*
Grieves, *pains ; afflicts.*
Greaves, *armor for the legs.*
Heel, *hind part of the foot.*
Heal, *to cure.*
Lean, *thin ; meager ; incline.*
Lien, *legal claim.*

ē

Flee, *to run away.*
Flea, *an insect.*
Lee, *side opposite to the wind.*
Lea, *meadow ; plain.*
Key, *that which locks.*
Quay, *a mole, or wharf.*
Lief, *willingly ; gladly.*
Leaf, *part of a plant.*
Leek, *sort of onion.*
Leak, *ooze ; run out.*

EXERCISE 385.

ē

Meed, *reward.*
Mead, *meadow ; a drink.*
Mean, *low ; base.*
Mien, *look ; aspect.*
Mesne, *middle ; intervening.*
Need, *want.*
*K*nead, *to work, as dough.*
Neal, *temper by heat.*
*K*neel, *to rest on the knees.*

ē

Lēach, *pass water through*
Leech, *a blood-sucker.* [*ashes.*
Peace, *rest ; quietness.*
Piece, *a part.*
Peak, *top ; summit.*
Pïque, *offense ; spite.*
Peel, *to strip off ; to skin.*
Peal, *loud sound.*

EXERCISE 386.

ē	ē
Queen, *consort of a king.*	Peer, *an equal; nobleman.*
Quean, *a worthless woman.*	Pier, *support of an arch.*
Reed, *plant; weaver's tool.*	Please, *give pleasure.*
Read, *to peruse.*	Pleas, *pleadings.*
Reek, *emit smoke or vapor.*	Sheer, *pure; unmixed.*
Wreak, *take vengeance.*	Shïre, *county, or district.*
See, *perceive by the eye.*	Shear, *clip with scissors.*
Sea, *great body of water.*	Sleeve, *covering for the arm.*
Seem, *appear.*	Sleave, *to part threads.*
Seam, *join by sewing.*	Steel, *hardened iron.*
Seize, *grasp.*	Steal, *to take by theft.*
Sees, *does see.*	Sweet, *agreeable to the taste.*
Seas, *more than one sea.*	Suïte, *train; series.*

EXERCISE 387.

ē	ē
Tēal, *a web-footed fowl.*	Ween, *think; deem.*
Teil, *lime-tree.*	Wean, *draw off; alienate.*
Teem, *be full; bring forth.*	Wheel, *circular frame.*
Team, *horses or oxen in harness.*	Wheal, *pustule.*
Week, *seven days.*	Leave, *quit; abandon.*
Weak, *feeble; infirm.*	Lieve, *gladly; willingly.*
Weel, *snare or trap for fish.*	Reeve, *bird; to pass a rope.*
Weal, *well-being; happiness.*	Reave, *take away; to rob.*

EXERCISE 388.

ē	ē
Cēil′ ing, *the inner roof.*	Ar rēar′, *what remains due.*
Seal ing, *fixing a seal.*	Ar riere, *last body of an army.*
Sen ior, *elder; older.*	De mean, *to behave; deport.*
Seign ior, *lord; title of honor.*	De mesne, *chief manor-place.*
Ve nus, *one of the planets.*	Dis creet, *prudent.*
Ve nous, *of the veins.*	Dis crete, *distinct; separate.*
Week ly, *once a week.*	Seem′ing, *appearing.*
Weak ly, *infirm; invalid.*	Seam ing, *making seams.*

EXERCISE 389.

ī	ī
Bīte, *press or crush with the teeth.*	Hīre, *wages ; to let.*
Bight, *a small bay.*	High er, *more high.*
Cite, *to summon ; repeat.*	Isle, *a small island.*
Sight, *a view ; scene.*	I'll, *I will.*
Site, *situation ; locality.*	Aisle, *passage in a church.*
Blite, *kind of plant.*	Mite, *minute insect.*
Blight, *to blast ; destroy.*	Might, *force ; power.*
Clime, *region ; climate.*	Nice, *neat ; dainty.*
Climb, *mount ; ascend.*	Gneiss, *a species of rock.*
Hīgh, *lofty ; elevated.*	Night, *from sunset to sunrise.*
Hie, *hasten ; run.*	Knight, *champion.*

EXERCISE 390.

ī	ī
Quīre, *twenty-four sheets of paper.*	Sīze, *bulk ; bigness.*
Choir, *body of singers.*	Siçe, *number six at dice.*
Rice, *esculent grain.*	Sighs, *does sigh ; moans.*
Riṣe, *act of rising ; ascent.*	Slight, *neglect.*
Ring, *circle ; a sound.*	Sleight, *a trick.*
Wring, *to twist.*	Tide, *flow of the sea.*
Rite, *ceremony.*	Tied, *bound ; fastened.*
Write, *trace letters with a pen.*	Find, *discover.*
Right, *just ; proper.*	Fined, *taxed.*
Wright, *a workman.*	Ap prize', *to value : rate.*
Sine, *line in mathematics.*	Apprise, *to give notice ; inform.*
Sign, *mark ; signal.*	In dite, *to compose.*
	In dict, *accuse in a court of law.*

EXERCISE 391.

ō	ō
Bōle, *body of a tree.*	Bōrne, *carried ; conveyed.*
Boll, *pod of a plant.*	Bourn, *limit ; boundary.*
Bore, *make a hole ; weary.*	Toad, *an animal.*
Boar, *the male of swine.*	Towed, *did tow.*
Blote, *to dry and smoke.*	Bow, *instrument to shoot arrows.*
Bloat, *to puff, or swell out.*	Beau, *man of dress.*

EXERCISE 392.

ō

Brōach, *pierce, as with a spit.*
Brooch, *breastpin.*

Course, *way; career.*
Coarse, *not fine; rough.*

Core, *heart; inner part.*
Corps, *body of troops.*

Cote, *pen; fold.*
Coat, *outer garment.*

Doe, *female deer.*
Dough, *unbaked paste.*

ō

Fōe, *enemy.*
Foh, *fie; word of contempt.*
Fore, *before.*
Four, *twice two.*
Fort, *strong place; fortress.*
Forte, *one's strong point.*
Forth, *forward.*
Fourth, *next after the third.*
Glome, *roundish head of flowers.*
Gloam, *to be sullen, or surly.*

EXERCISE 393.

ō

Glōze, *to flatter.*
Glows, *does glow; burns.*

Groan, *sound uttered from pain.*
Grown, *arrived at full size.*

Horde, *tribe or clan.*
Hoard, *to lay up; amass.*

Ho, *a word to excite attention.*
Hoe, *tool used in farming.*

ō

Hōle, *hollow place; cavity.*
Whole, *all; entire.*

Hose, *stockings.*
Hoes, *more than one hoe.*

Lone, *solitary.*
Loan, *to lend.*

Lo, *look; behold.*
Low, *not high; humble.*

Lore, *learning.*
Low' er, *less high.*

EXERCISE 394.

ō

Mōan, *lament; bewail.*
Mown, *cut down, as grass.*

Mote, *fine particle.*
Moat, *ditch for defense.*

More, *greater in amount.*
Mow er, *one that mows.*

No, *nay; not any.*
Know, *have knowledge of.*

ō

Nome, *province or district.*
Gnome, *spirit; goblin.*

Ore, *metal in fossil state.*
Oar, *sort of paddle for rowing.*
O'er, *over; above.*
Oh, *word of surprise, or pain.*
Owe, *to be in debt.*

Pole, *rod; long stick.*
Poll, *the head; to register.*

EXERCISE 395.

ō	ō
Pōre, *minute hole.*	Rōte, *routine; kind of guitar.*
Pour, *to cause to issue, as water.*	Wrote, *did write.*
Port, *harbor; haven.*	Shone, *did shine.*
Porte, *Turkish Court.*	Shown, *held out to view.*
Rōde, *did ride.*	Slōe, *wild plum.*
Road, *way; route.*	Slow, *not fast; sluggish.*
Row ed, *did row.*	Sole, *only; bottom of the foot.*
Roar, *cry aloud.*	Soul, *immortal part of man.*
Row er, *one that rows.*	So, *thus; in like manner.*
Roe, *female of the hart.*	Sow, *scatter seed.*
Row, *a rank; to propel by oars.*	Sew (so), *join with a needle.*

EXERCISE 396.

ō	ō
Sōre, *wound; ulcer.*	Tōle, *to draw; to allure.*
Soar, *mount up; ascend.*	Toll, *tax; to ring, as a bell.*
Sow er, *one that sows seed.*	Gored, *pierced, as with a horn.*
Thrōe, *extreme pain.*	Gourd, *kind of plant.*
Throw, *cast; hurl.*	Ode, *song; hymn.*
Throne, *seat of a monarch.*	Owed, *did owe.*
Thrown, *cast; hurled.*	Roam, *wander; stray.*
Toe, *part of the foot.*	Rome, *name of a city.*
Tow, *coarse part of flax.*	Bold' er, *more bold.*
Told, *did tell.*	Bould er, *large, round stone.*
Toled, *did tole; allured.*	Ho ly, *sacred: divine.*
Tolled, *did tax; did ring.*	Whol ly, *entirely.*

EXERCISE 397.

ū	ū
Dūe, *what is owed; debt.*	Uşe, *to employ.*
Dew, *moisture.*	Ewes, *female sheep.*
Hue, *color; an outcry.*	Flue, *smoke-passage.*
Hew, *to cut.*	Flew, *did fly.*
Blue, *a color.*	Mūle, *a mongrel animal.*
Blew, *did blow.*	Mewl, *to cry, as a child.*

EXERCISE 398.

ū

Mūse, *to think.*
Mews, *cages for birds.*
New, *fresh; not old.*
Knew, *did know.*
Slue, *to turn about the axis.*
Slew, *did slay.*

ū

Yoū, *thyself.*
Yew, *a tree.*
Pu′ ny, *small; feeble.*
Puis ne, *inferior in rank.*
Mu′ cus, *a slimy fluid.*
Mu cous, *slimy; like mucus.*

EXERCISE 399.

ȳ

Bȳ, *near; through.*
Buy, *purchase.*
Dye, *color; tinge.*
Die, *to expire.*
Rye, *sort of grain.*
Wry, *twisted; turned to one side.*
Lyre, *musical instrument.*
Li′ ar, *one that lies.*
Thyme, *a plant.*
Time, *measure of duration.*
Lye, *water passed thro' ashes.*
Lie, *untruth; falsehood.*

ȳ

Eȳe, *organ of sight.*
I, *myself.*
Gybe, *to shift a boom-sail.*
Gibe, *to mock; to jeer.*
Rhyme, *sameness of sound.*
Rime, *hoar frost.*
Tyre, *name of a city.*
Tire, *to fatigue.*
Dy′ ing, *expiring; perishing.*
Dye ing, *coloring.*
Eye let, *small hole for lace or cord.*
Is let, *a small island.*

EXERCISE 400.

ă

Ab, *a month in the Jewish year.*
Abb, *yarn for the warp.*
Adz, *a cooper's tool.*
Adds, *does add; joins.*
Dam, *mother of brutes.*
Damn, *condemn.*
Dram, *drink of spirituous liquor.*
Drachm, *eighth of an ounce.*
Bad, *evil; wicked.*
Bade, *did bid; ordered.*

ă

Jăg, *small load.*
Jagg, *to notch, or indent.*
Jam, *press; conserve of fruits.*
Jamb, *side piece of a chimney.*
Lax, *loose; remiss.*
Lacks, *does lack; wants.*
Nag, *small horse.*
Knag, *knot in wood.*
Nap, *a short sleep; doze.*
Knap, *to bite; a hillock.*

EXERCISE 401.

ă	ă
Răck, *engine of torture.*	Căl' lus, *a hardness of the skin.*
Wrack, *sea-weed.*	Cal lous, *hardened; unfeeling.*
Rap, *slight blow; to strike.*	Can non, *large gun.*
Wrap, *fold up.*	Can on, *a law, or rule.*
Tax, *rate imposed; duty.*	Can vas, *coarse cloth.*
Tacks, *small nails.*	Can vass, *to discuss; examine.*
An' il, *a shrub.*	Pan el, *a jury roll.*
An ile, *old-womanish.*	Pan nel, *a rustic saddle.*
Faç et, *a little face.*	Pact, *league; contract.*
Fas cet, *an iron rod; puntil.*	Pack ed, *did pack; put up.*
Cal id, *hot; burning.*	Gal' i pot, *a white resin.*
Cal lid, *cun ning; crafty.*	Gal li pot, *pot for medicines.*

EXERCISE 402.

ĕ	ĕ
Bĕll, *a hollow sounding vessel.*	Cĕnse, *a public tax.*
Belle, *gay young lady.*	Sense, *power of perception.*
Blend, *mix; mingle.*	Cent, *copper coin.*
Blende, *ore of zinc; mock-lead.*	Sent, *did send.*
	Scent, *odor; perfume.*
Bred, *brought up; begotten.*	Jest, *joke.*
Bread, *article of food.*	Gest, *deed; action.*
Cell, *small close room.*	Guest, *visitor.*
Sell, *to part with for a price.*	Guessed, *did guess.*

EXERCISE 403.

ĕ	ĕ
Lĕd, *did lead; conducted.*	Rest, *peace; freedom from toil.*
Lead, *a soft metal.*	Wrest, *distort; pervert.*
Red, *a color.*	Retch, *effort to vomit.*
Read, *did read; perused.*	Wretch, *miserable creature.*
Reck, *care; heed.*	Step, *pace; walk.*
Wreck, *destroy.*	Steppe, *barren plain.*

EXERCISE 404.

ĕ	ĕ
Bĕr' ry, *a small fruit.*	Wĕath' er, *state of the air.*
Bu ry, *to cover; to inter.*	Weth er, *a sheep.*
Les sen, *to decrease.*	As sent', *to agree to.*
Les son, *a task; a precept.*	As cent, *a rising ground.*
Ces sion, *a giving up; a grant.*	Con cent, *concord of sounds.*
Ses sion, *a sitting in council.*	Con sent, *assent; free-will.*
Pen cil, *instrument to draw with.*	In ten' tion, *design; purpose.*
Pen sile, *hanging.*	In ten sion, *a stretching.*

EXERCISE 405.

ĭ	ĭ
In, *within.*	Sink, *to settle down.*
Inn, *a tavern.*	Cinque, *five.*
Bin, *a box; chest.*	Bit, *part of a thing.*
Been, *existed.*	Bitt, *frame to fasten a cable.*
Gild, *overlay with gold.*	Kĭll, *slay; murder.*
Guild, *a society.*	Kiln, *oven to bake brick in.*
Gilt, *overlaid with gold.*	Hist, *hush; be silent.*
Guilt, *crime; fault.*	Hiss ed, *did hiss.*

EXERCISE 406.

ĭ	ĭ
Mist, *water in very fine drops.*	Gild' er, *one who gilds.*
Miss ed, *did miss; failed.*	Guild er, *a Dutch coin.*
Nit, *egg of an insect.*	Griz zly, *somewhat gray.*
Knit, *to weave with needles.*	Gris ly, *frightful; hideous.*
Stick, *short piece of wood.*	Per mis' ci ble, *that may be mixed.*
Stich, *line of poetry.*	Per mis si ble, *allowable.*
Dis' cus, *a quoit.*	In cĭp i ence, *commencement.*
Dis cous, *broad; flat; wide.*	In sip i ence, *want of wisdom.*
Fil ter, *to strain.*	In cis ion, *a cutting into.*
Phil ter, *a love potion; charm.*	In sĭ tion, *a setting in; graft.*

EXERCISE 407.

ŏ

Lock, *to fasten with a lock.*
Lough, *a lake.*

Hock, *a kind of wine.*
Hough, *lower part of the thigh.*

Not, *a word of denial; no.*
*K*not, *a tie; to tie.*

Sŏr′ rel, *a plant.*
Sor el, *a buck of the third year.*

Ton sil, *gland in the throat.*
Ton sile, *that may be clipped.*

ŏ

Pŏl′ y pus, *a thing with many feet, or roots.*
Pol y pous, *like the polypus.*

Sar cŏph′ a gus, *stone coffin.*
Sar coph a gous, *flesh-eating.*

The oc′ ra cy, *government immediately under God.*
The oc ra sy, *mixture of the worship of different gods.*

EXERCISE 408.

ŭ

Sŭn, *orb of light and heat.*
Sȯn, *a male child.*

Dun, *ask payment; a color.*
Dȯne, *finished; completed.*

Dust, *fine particles of dry earth.*
Dȯst, *performest.*

Just, *right; proper.*
Joust, *tilt; mock-fight.*

ŭ

Plŭm, *a kind of fruit.*
Plumb, *upright; erect.*

Ruff, *plaited linen for the neck.*
Rough, *uneven.*

Chuff, *a clownish person.*
Chough, *a fowl.*

Rung, *did ring; sounded.*
*W*rung, *did ring; twisted.*

EXERCISE 409.

ŭ

Mum, *a malt-liquor; silent.*
Mumm, *to mask.*

Skull, *bone inclosing the brain.*
Scull, *to impel a boat by an oar at the stern.*

But, *on the contrary; except.*
Butt, *to strike with the head.*

Sun′ less, *without the sun.*
Sȯn less, *without a son.*

ŭ

Cŭd′ dle, *to lie snug, or close.*
Cud le, *a small sea-fish.*

Sum, *amount.*
Sȯme, *not all; certain ones.*

Nun, *a female recluse.*
Nȯne, *no one.*

Coŭs in, *child of uncle or aunt.*
Coz en, *to cheat.*

Sut′ tle, *net weight.*
Su*b* tle, *sly; artful.*

EXERCISE 410.

ȳ

Lȳnx, *animal of the cat kind.*
Links, *parts of a chain.*
Hymn, *a sacred song.*
Him, *that one.*
Wynn, *kind of truck, or carriage.*
Win, *to gain by contest.*
Cyst, *sac; bladder.*
Sist, *to stay proceedings.*
Cyn′ic al, *snarling; captious.*
Sin i cal, *pertaining to a sine.*

ȳ

Hȳp, *low spirits.*
Hip, *joint of the thigh.*
Styx, *a fabled river.*
Sticks, *pieces of wood.*
Lyn, *a waterfall.*
Lin, *to yield; to cease.*
Pȳx, *a box.*
Picks, *does pick; chooses.*
Cyg′ net, *a young swan.*
Sig net, *a seal.*

EXERCISE 411.

â

Bâre, *nude; naked.*
Bear, *an animal; to suffer.*
Fare, *food; cost of a passage.*
Fair, *clear; comely.*
Glare, *a dazzling light.*
Glair, *the white of an egg.*
Ware, *merchandise; cautious.*
Wear, *to waste by friction.*
Hare, *an animal.*
Hair, *filament from the skin.*

â

Pâre, *to cut; to trim.*
Pair, *a couple.*
Pear, *a kind of fruit.*
Stare, *to gaze.*
Stair, *a step for going up.*
Tare, *allowance.*
Tear, *to rend; to sunder.*
Par′ ed, *did pare; trimmed.*
Pair ed, *joined in pairs.*
Glar ed, *dazzled.*
Glair ed, *smeared with glair.*

EXERCISE 412.

ä

Härt, *a male deer.*
Heart, *the vital part; the core.*
Ark, *a chest; close vessel.*
Arc, *part of a circle.*
Barb, *down of plants; beard.*
Barbe, *leather armor for horses.*
Mar′ shal, *chief; to range in order.*
Mar tial, *warlike; brave.*

ȧ

Cȧsk, *a vessel for liquors.*
Casque, *armor for the head.*
Cast, *to throw, or hurl.*
Caste, *a tribe, or clan.*
Draft, *to outline; to sketch.*
Draught, *a drawing; a drink.*
Past, *not present; ended.*
Pass ed, *did pass.*

EXERCISE 413.

a̤

Ba̤ll, *a round body.*
Bawl, *to cry or speak aloud.*
All, *the whole; total.*
Awl, *a tool to pierce with.*
Awn, *the beard of corn.*
Auln, *a French measure; an ell.*
Bald, *without hair.*
Bawled, *did bawl; cried aloud.*
Aught, *anything.*
Ought, *in duty bound.*

a̤

Ca̤ll, *to name; to summon.*
Caul, *a membrane.*
Cause, *reason; motive.*
Caws, *does caw.*
Cauf, *a box for fish in water.*
Cough, *convulsion of the lungs.*
Cawk, *limestone.*
Calk, *to stop the seams of ships.*
Ward, *guard; custody.*
Warred, *did war; fought.*

EXERCISE 414.

a̤

Ha̤ll, *entrance; a large room.*
Haul, *to drag forcibly.*
Pall, *covering for the dead.*
Pawl, *short bar of wood, or iron.*
Pause, *to stop; cease.*
Paws, *feet of beasts.*
Clause, *part of a sentence.*
Claws, *hooked nails of animals.*
Wall, *a fence of stone or brick.*
Waul, *to cry as a cat.*

a̤

Ga̤ll, *bile; a bitter substance.*
Gaul, *ancient name of France.*
Fawn, *a young deer.*
Faun, *fabled deity of the woods.*
Haw, *berry of the hawthorn.*
Haugh, *a little, low meadow.*
Salt′ er, *more salt; one who salts.*
Psalt er, *the Book of Psalms.*

EXERCISE 415.

ê

Thêre, *in that place.*
Their, *of them.*
Hēir, *one that inherits.*
Ere, *before.*
Eyre, *court of circuit judges.*
Air, *fluid we breathe.*
Heir ed, *inherited.*
Air ed, *exposed to the air.*

ẽ

Sẽrge, *a woolen stuff.*
Sûrge, *wave; billow.*
Berth, *place to sleep in a ship.*
Birth, *act of coming into life.*
Earn, *deserve by labor.*
Urn, *vessel for liquids, etc*
Vers ed, *well skilled.*
Verst, *a Russian measure.*

EXERCISE 416.

o͞o and o͝o	ṳ
Co͞om, *coal-dust; soot.*	Grṳme, *clotted blood.*
Coomb, *four bushels.*	Groom, *one that tends horses.*
Hoop, *ring; circular band.*	Rude, *rough; uncivil.*
Whoop, *shout; outcry.*	Rued, *did rue.*
Droop, *sink, or hang down.*	Rood, *fourth of an acre.*
Drṳpe, *a pulpy fruit.*	Brṳte, *a beast.*
o͝o	Bruit, *to noise abroad.*
Wo͝od, *material of trees.*	Cru′ el, *inhuman.*
Would, *willed;* Pret. *of will.*	Crew el, *a ball of yarn.*

EXERCISE 417.

û	ou
Fûr, *fine soft hair.*	Flour, *fine part of ground [grain.*
Fir, *a kind of tree.*	Flow er, *a blossom.*
Purl, *to flow with a gentle [noise.*	Foul, *impure; dirty.*
Pearl, *a gem.*	Fowl, *a bird.*
Surf, *swell of the sea.*	Bough, *branch of a tree.*
Serf, *a slave; servant.*	Bow, *bend down; stoop.*
Bur′ row, *a hole in the ground.*	Fouler, *more foul.*
Bor ough, *a corporate town.*	Fowl er, *a bird-catcher; [sportsman.*

SECTION XVIII.

WORDS NEARLY ALIKE IN SOUND.

EXERCISE 418.

ā	ā
Lā′ va, *matter from a volcano.*	Rā′ zor, *instrument to shave.*
La ver, *vessel for washing.*	Rais er, *one that raises.*
Gla cie̤r, *broad field of ice.*	Sa vor, *taste; odor.*
Gla zier, *one that puts in glass.*	Sāv er, *one that saves.*
Na val, *relating to ships.*	A bel, *a man's name.*
Na vel, *central part; middle.*	A ble, *having power.*
A cre, 160 *sq. rods of land.*	As sāy′, *to test, as metals.*
A chor, *scald-head.*	Es say, *to try; attempt.*

EXERCISE 419.

ē	ē
Gē' nus, *a sort, or kind.*	Bē' tel, *a species of pepper.*
Gen ius, *aptitude; talent.*	Bee tle, *wooden mallet; insect.*
Pæ an, *song of triumph.*	Cease, *stop; desist.*
Pæ on, *a poetic foot.*	Seize, *lay hold of.*
E ther, *refined air; a fluid.*	Se rous, *thin; watery.*
Ei ther, *one or the other.*	Se ri ous, *grave; earnest.*
E gret, *a heron.*	De cēase', *death.*
E gri ot, *a kind of cherry.*	Dis ease, *sickness.*

EXERCISE 420.

ī	ī
Pī'lot, *steersman; guide.*	Brī'dal, *relating to a bride.*
Pi late, *a man's name.*	Bri dle, *head-rein; curb.*
I dle, *slothful.*	Mi ner, *one that mines.*
I dol, *image for worship.*	Mi nor, *less; under age.*
I dyl, *pastoral poem.*	Pri or, *former; previous.*
Di vī'sor, *number that divides.*	Pri er, *one that pries.*
De vis or, *a testator.*	Vi al, *small glass bottle.*
De vis er, *one that contrives.*	Vi ol. *musical instrument.*

EXERCISE 421.

ō	ō
Pō'lar, *relating to the poles.*	Clōse, *to shut up; end.*
Poll er, *one that polls.*	Clothes, *articles of dress.*
Po tion, *drink; draught.*	Tome, *a volume.*
Por tion, *share; part.*	Tomb, *a sepulcher.*
Po sy, *motto; nosegay.*	Fore most, *most advanced.*
Po e sy, *poetry; verse.*	Fore màst, *mast near the bow.*
Po ta ble, *fit to drink.*	Fo"e man, *chief man.*
Port a ble, *able to be carried.*	Foe man, *enemy.*

EXERCISE 422.

ū	ȳ
Dū' al, *relating to two.*	Cȳ' press, *a forest tree.*
Du el, *fight between two.*	Cȳ prus, *crape; an island.*
Sut ure, *act of sewing; seam.*	Ty phon, *an evil spirit.*
Suit or, *one that sues; lover.*	Ty phoon', *a whirlwind.*
Hu mer al, *the shoulder.*	Dry as, *a wood-nymph.*
Hu mor al, *relating to humors.*	Dry os, *kind of mistletoe.*
E lu'sive, *tending to elude*	Dry ad, *a wood-nymph.*
Il lu sive, *making a false show.*	Dri ed, *did dry.*

EXERCISE 423.

ă

Trăck, *trace; footstep.*
Tract, *region; district.*
Ab′ bey, *a monastery.*
Ab ba, *father.*
An gor, *intense pain.*
An ger, *passion, vexation.*
An̲k er, *measure for liquids.*
Anch or, *hold-fast for ships.*
Lăt in, *a language.*
Lat ten, *plates of iron tinned.*

ă

Băl let, *a comic dance.*
Bal lot, *ticket for voting.*
Bar on, *a rank in nobility.*
Bar ren, *sterile; unfruitful.*
Cap tor, *one that captures.*
Capt ure, *to take as a prize.*
Car at, *weight of four grains.*
Car rot, *a garden plant.*
Gam ble, *to game.*
Gam bol, *to leap and skip.*

EXERCISE 424.

ă

Măn′ner, *mode; way; fashion.*
Man or, *a dominion of a lord.*
Mat rass, *a chemical vessel.*
Mat tress, *a quilted bed.*
Pal ate, *the roof of the mouth.*
Pal let, *a small bed.*
Rab bet, *joint; to join boards.*
Rab bit, *an animal.*
An a lyst, *one that analyzes.*
An nal ist, *a writer of annals.*

ă

Stăt′ue, *image of wood, stone.*
Stat ute, *a law.*
Trav el, *to journey.*
Trav ail, *to toil; to suffer* [*pain.*
Cal en dar, *a register of times.*
Cal en der, *a hot press.*
Cap i tal, *chief; a large letter.*
Cap i tol, *legislature house.*
Rad i cal, *pertaining to a root.*
Rad i cle, *young root; germ.*

EXERCISE 425.

ĕ

Sĕll′er, *one that sells.*
Cel lar, *room under a house.*
Med al, *metal shaped like coin.*
Med dle, *to interfere.*
Met al, *mineral, as gold, etc.*
Met tle, *spirit; courage.*
Ped al, *pertaining to the feet.*
Ped dle, *to go about to sell.*

ĕ

Tĕn′or, *stamp; character.*
Ten ure, *hold; claim.*
De scent′, *a coming down.*
Dis sent, *disagreement.*
E lect′ or, *one that elects.*
E lec tre, *amber.*
Preç′ e dent, *going before.*
Preș i dent, *one who presides.*

EXERCISE 426.

ĭ

Mĭs' sĭle, *a thing thrown.*
Mis sal, *prayer-book; ritual.*
Pil low, *cushion for the head.*
Pil lar, *a column.*
Rig or, *stiffness; severity.*
Rig ger, *one that rigs vessels.*
Pis til, *part of a flower.*
Pis tol, *small fire-arm.*
Pis tole, *a gold coin.*
Ca lĭd' i ty, *heart; warmth.*
Cal lid i ty, *skill; cunning.*
E lĭc it, *to draw out.*
Il lic it, *unlawful.*

ĭ

Bĭn' na cle, *compass-box.*
Bin o cle, *kind of telescope.*
Lic o rice, *root of sweet taste.*
Lick er ish, *dainty; delicate.*
Lit er al, *pertaining to letters.*
Lit to ral, *relating to the shore.*
Prin ci pal, *chief; main.*
Prin ci ple, *law, or rule.*
Mil le na ry, *thousand years.*
Mil li ner y, *bonnets, ribbons.*
E lis'ion, *act of cutting off.*
E lys i an, *of Elysium; happy.*

EXERCISE 427.

ŏ

Cŏl' lar, *thing worn round the neck.*
Chol er, *bile; anger.*
Prof it, *gain; advantage.*
Proph et, *one that predicts.*
Con dor, *a species of vulture.*
Cond er, *helmsman's director.*
A pos' tle, *messenger.*
A pos til, *marginal note.*
De pos it a ry, *a trustee.*
De pos it o ry, *place of deposit.*

ŏ

Hŏn'or a ry, *conferring honor.*
On er a ry, *burdensome.*
Com pli ment, *a civility.*
Com ple ment, *full sum.*
Proph e cy, *prediction.*
Proph e sy, *to predict.*
Chron i cle, *register of events.*
Chron i cal, *relating to time.*
Pop u lous, *full of people.*
Pop u lace, *the people.*

EXERCISE 428.

ŭ

Cŭll' er, *one that culls.*
Còl or, *hue; dye; tint.*
Suck er, *that which sucks.*
Suc cor, *aid; help.*
But tress, *prop; support.*
But ter is, *tool for paring hoofs.*
Pum ice, *substance thrown from volcanoes.*
Pom ace, *crushed apples.*

ŭ

Scŭlp' tor, *maker of statues.*
Sculp ture, *statuary.*
Fa cun' di ty, *ready speech.*
Fe cun di ty, *fruitfulness.*

y̆

Cy̆m' bal, *musical instrument.*
Sym bol, *type; emblem.*

EXERCISE 429.

ä

Mär' tin, *a swallow.*
Mar ten, *kind of weasel.*
Far ther, *more distant.*
Fa ther, *male parent.*
Balm, *a healing ointment.*
Barm, *yeast.*
Parse, *analyze sentences.*
Påss, *move by; go on.*

å

Lånch, *to hurl as a spear.*
Läunch, *slide, or shove off.*
Pas tor, *shepherd; minister.*
Pas ture, *grazing-ground.*
Cast er, *a cruet; a vial.*
Cas tor, *kind of beaver.*
Pass a ble, *able to be passed.*
Pas si ble, *able to be felt.*

EXERCISE 430.

a̤

Au' ḡer, *a boring tool.*
Au gur, *to predict; forebode.*
La̤wn, *open space of ground.*
Lôrn, *forsaken; lonely.*
Laud, *praise.*
Lôrd, *master; nobleman.*
Au ri cle, *external ear.*
Or a cle,* *response of a deity.*

ẽ

De s̱ẽrt', *forsake.*
Des̱ s̱ert, *last course at table.*
E merge, *come forth; rise.*
Im merge, *plunge into.*
Earn'ing, *meriting by service.*
Urn ing, *putting into an urn.*
Vẽr' tic al, *directly over head.*
Vôr tic al, *like a whirlpool.*

EXERCISE 431.

ĩ

Vĩr' tue, *moral goodness.*
Vir tṳ', *love of the fine arts.*
First, *foremost.*
Fūst, *strong musty smell.*

û

Bûrst, *break open.*
Bust, *upper half of the body.*
Durst, *dared; ventured.*
Dust, *fine particles of earth.*
Cur rant, *a fruit; dried grape.*
Cur rent, *flowing; passing.*

ô

Sôrt, *kind; species.*
Sought, *searched after.*
Stork, *large wading bird.*
Sta̤lk, *walk pompously.*
For' mer ly, *in time past.*
For mal ly, *in formal manner.*
Ord nance, *cannon; mortars.*
Or di nance, *law; statute.*
Or don nance, *arrangement.*
Cor po ral, *relating to the body.*
Cor pō' re al, *having a body.*

---

* The *o* in *oracle* is the regular ŏ (*short*, not ô).

SECTION XIX.

ANALYSIS OF WORDS.

That part of a derivative word which contains the principal idea, is called the ROOT, or RADICAL. Thus TRACT, in the word EXTRACT, is the radical part, and means to *draw*.

The syllable EX, which comes *before* the radical, is called a PREFIX, and means *out;* so that the two combined signify to *draw out.*

If now to the word EXTRACT we add the syllable ED, which is called a SUFFIX, and means *did*, we shall have EX TRACT ED, which, putting the meaning of the several parts together, may be defined *did draw out.*

Thus the meaning of each part is disclosed, and the whole satisfactorily explained. This mode of dealing with words, in order to ascertain their full and exact signification, is called, ANALYSIS.

It should be added, that the roots or radicals, in English, are of *two kinds*. Some of them are entire, independent words, and may stand in a sentence without being combined with any prefix or suffix. Thus, ACT, JOIN, SOFT, are of this kind, and are hence called *separable radicals.*

But there are many which, like JECT, in EJECT, CLUDE, in EXCLUDE, and TEP, in TEPID, can never appear *alone.* These have a separate and independent *meaning*, like the others, and may be defined in the same manner; but, because of their always forming only a *part* of a word, they are called *inseparable radicals.*

PREFIXES.

In the Exercises following, the PREFIX, and the RADICAL, each with the proper definition *underneath*, occupy the first and second columns respectively. In the third column, they are put together as one word, and in the fourth, the DERIVATIVE word thus formed, is defined by bringing together the definitions previously given of the parts taken separately.

EXERCISE 432.

PREFIXES.	RADICALS.	DERIVATIVES.	DEFINITIONS OF DERIVATIVES.
Ab *from; away.*	duct *lead.*	**Ab duct',**	*to lead from, or away.*
Ad *to; at; near.*	join *add.*	**Ad join',**	*to join to.*
Ana *up; again.*	lyze *loosen.*	**An' a lyze,**	*to loosen up; resolve into elements.*
Ante *before.*	cedent *going.*	**An te cēd' ent,**	*going before.*
Anti *against.*	pathy *feeling.*	**An tip' a thy,**	*feeling against; ill-will.*
Be *by; over; make.*	daub *smear.*	**Be daub',**	*smear over.*
Bene *well; good.*	factor *doer.*	**Ben e fac' tor,**	*one who does good.*

EXERCISE 433.

Circum *around.*	fluent *flowing.*	**Cir cum' flu ent,**	*flowing around.*
Cis *on this side.*	alpine *of the Alps.*	**Cis al' pine,**	*on this side the Alps.*
Con *with; together.*	voke *call.*	**Con voke',**	*to call together.*
Contra *against.*	vene *go.*	**Con tra vene',**	*to go against; oppose.*
De *from; down.*	flect *turn.*	**De flect',**	*to turn from, or aside.*
Dis *apart; away.*	miss *send.*	**Dis miss',**	*to send away; let go.*
Ex *out; out of.*	pel, *drive.*	**Ex pel,**	*drive out.*

EXERCISE 434.

PREFIXES.	RADICALS.	DERIVATIVES.	DEFINITIONS OF DERIVATIVES.
En *in; to make.*	**wrap** *fold.*	**En wrap′,**	*to fold in.*
Extra *beyond.*	**vagant** *straying.*	**Ex trav′ a gant,**	*straying beyond limits.*
Fore *before.*	**doom** *condemn.*	**Fore doom′,**	*to condemn beforehand.*
Hemi *half.*	**sphere** *globe.*	**Hem′ i sphere,**	*half a sphere.*
In *in; into.*	**cise** *cut.*	**In cise′,**	*to cut in, or into.*
Inter *between.*	**jacent** *lying.*	**In ter ja′ cent,**	*lying between.*
Intro *within.*	**spect** *look.*	**In tro spect′,**	*to look within.*

EXERCISE 435.

PREFIXES.	RADICALS.	DERIVATIVES.	DEFINITIONS OF DERIVATIVES.
Mis *wrong.*	**guide** *lead.*	**Mis guide′,**	*to guide wrong.*
Male *evil; wrong.*	**factor** *doer.*	**Mal e fac′ tor,**	*one who does evil.*
Ob *in front; against.*	**struct** *pile up.*	**Ob sruct′,**	*to pile up in front of; to oppose.*
Out *beyond.*	**last** *endure.*	**Out last′,**	*to last beyond.*
Over *above; beyond.*	**value** *prize.*	**O ver val′ ue,**	*to prize beyond.*
Per *through.*	**forate** *bore.*	**Per′ fo rate,**	*to bore through.*
Post *after; afterwards.*	**pone** *put.*	**Post pone′,**	*put after; defer.*

EXERCISE 436.

PREFIXES.	RADICALS.	DERIVATIVES.	DEFINITIONS OF DERIVATIVES.
Pre *before.*	**cursive** *running.*	**Pre cur′ sive,**	*running before.*
Preter *beyond; past.*	**legal** *lawful.*	**Pre ter le′ gal,**	*beyond the legal.*
Pro *before; forth.*	**duce** *lead.*	**Pro duce′,**	*to lead, or bring forth.*
Re *again; back.*	**view** *see.*	**Re view′,**	*to view again.*
Retro *backwards.*	**grade** *step.*	**Ret′ ro grade,**	*to go backwards.*
Se *aside; apart.*	**cede** *go.*	**Se cede′,**	*to go aside, or apart.*
Semi *half.*	**nude** *naked.*	**Sem i nude′,**	*half naked.*

EXERCISE 437.

PREFIXES.	RADICALS.	DERIVATIVES.	DEFINITIONS OF DERIVATIVES.
Sub *under*	**side** *sit; settle.*	**Sub side′,**	*to settle under; sink.*
Subter *under.*	**fluous** *flowing.*	**Sub ter′ flu ous,**	*flowing under.*
Super *over; above.*	**natant** *swimming.*	**Su per na′ tant,**	*swimming above.*
Syn *with; together.*	**thesis** *act of putting.*	**Syn′ the sis,**	*a putting together.*
Sus *up; upward.*	**tain** *hold.*	**Sus tain′,**	*to hold up; support.*
Trans *across; over.*	**port** *carry.*	**Trans port′,**	*to carry over.*
Up *above; on high.*	**lift** *raise.*	**Up lift′,**	*to lift on high.*
Ultra *beyond.*	**mundane** *worldly.*	**Ul tra mun′dane,**	*beyond the worldly, or what pertains to this world.*
Un *not.*	**wise** *prudent.*	**Un wise′,**	*not wise; imprudent.*
With *against; aside.*	**stand** *hold ground.*	**With stand′,**	*to stand against.*

EXERCISE 438.

Be* *deprive of.*	**head** *chief part.*	**Be head′,**	*to deprive of head; put to death.*
Con *completely.*	**vert** *turn.*	**Con vert,**	*to turn completely; renew; transform.*
De *deprive of.*	**fame** *character.*	**De fame,**	*to deprive of character; to slander.*
Dis *deprive of.*	**arm** *weapon.*	**Dis arm,**	*to deprive of arms.*
Dis *not.*	**credit** *trust.*	**Dis cred it,**	*not to credit; to disbelieve.*
Dis *entirely.*	**sever** *to part.*	**Dis sev er,**	*to sever entirely.*
In *not.*	**sane** *sound.*	**In sane,**	*not sound in mind; deranged.*
Un *deprive of.*	**curl** *ringlet.*	**Un curl,**	*to deprive of curls; loose from ringlets.*
Un *not.*	**current** *passing.*	**Un cur′ rent,**	*not current; not passing.*

* The examples in Exercise 438, are to illustrate certain *special* meanings of some of the Prefixes. Thus, *Be*, in *Behead*, means *to deprive of*, and is then said to be *Privative*; so *De*, in *Defame*, and *Dis*, in *Disarm*.

When a Prefix signifies *not*, as in *dislike* (*not* to like), it is said to be *Negative*. When it merely adds force to the natural meaning of the radical, as *Con*, in *Convert*, it is said to be *Intensive*, and may be rendered by such words, as *very*, *completely*, *entirely*, etc.

SECTION XX.

DIFFERENT FORMS OF SOME OF THE PREFIXES.

Some of the Prefixes have a variety of forms. Thus, AD has no less than ten, as *ad, af, ag, al, an, ap, ar, as, at, a.* These changes of form in the Prefixes are all made for the sake of euphony.

EXERCISE 439.

Forms of AD.

PREFIXES.	RADICALS.	DERIVATIVES.	DEFINITIONS OF DERIVATIVES.
Ad *to.*	duce *lead.*	**Ad duce'**	*lead to; bring forward.*
Af *to.*	fix *fasten.*	**Af fix,**	*fasten to; subjoin.*
Ag *to.*	group *gather.*	**Ag group,**	*gather to; bring together.*
Al *to.*	lot *assign.*	**Al lot,**	*assign to; distribute.*
An *to*	nex *join.*	**An nex,**	*join to; adjoin.*
Ap *to.*	pend *hang.*	**Ap pend,**	*hang to; attach.*
Ar *to.*	range *row.*	**Ar range,**	*range to; put in order.*
As *to.*	sume *take.*	**As sume,**	*take to, or upon one's self.*
At *to.*	tract *draw.*	**At tract,**	*draw to; allure.*
A *to.*	mount *rise.*	**A mount,**	*rise to; come up to.*

EXERCISE 440.

Forms of CON.

PREFIXES.	RADICALS.	DERIVATIVES.	DEFINITIONS OF DERIVATIVES.
Con *together.*	nect *link.*	**Con nect',**	*to link together.*
Cog *together.*	nate *born.*	**Cog' nate,**	*born together; akin.*
Col *together.*	lect *gather.*	**Col lect',**	*to gather together.*
Com *together.*	pact *drive.*	**Com pact,**	*drive together; compress.*
Cor *together.*	ri val *compete.*	**Cor ri' val,**	*to compete together.*
Co *together.*	erce *force.*	**Co erce',**	*force together; compel.*

EXERCISE 441.

Forms of OB.

PREFIXES.	RADICALS.	DERIVATIVES.	DEFINITIONS OF DERIVATIVES.
Ob *in front.*	**ject,** *throw.*	**Ob ject',**	*throw in front of; oppose.*
Oc *in front.*	**cur** *run.*	**Oc cur,**	*run in front of; come to pass.*
Of *in front.*	**fer** *bear.*	**Of fer,**	*bear in front of; present.*
Op *in front.*	**pose** *put.*	**Op pose',**	*put in front of, or against.*
Os *in front.*	**tentation** *act of holding.*	**Os ten ta'tion,**	*act of holding in front; display.*

EXERCISE 442.

Forms of SUB and TRANS.

PREFIXES.	RADICALS.	DERIVATIVES.	DEFINITIONS OF DERIVATIVES.
Sub *under.*	**due** *lead.*	**Sub due',**	*lead, or bring under.*
Suc *under.*	**cumb** *lie.*	**Suc cumb,**	*lie under; yield.*
Suf *under.*	**fer** *bear.*	**Suf fer,**	*bear up under; endure.*
Sug *under.*	**gest** *bring.*	**Sug gest',**	*bring under notice; to hint.*
Sup *under.*	**press** *force.*	**Sup press,**	*press under; put down.*
Trans *over.*	**gress** *step.*	**Trans gress,**	*step over; violate.*
Tres *over.*	**pass** *step.*	**Tres'pass,**	*step over; sin against.*

EXERCISE 443.

Forms of IN and INTER.

PREFIXES.	RADICALS.	DERIVATIVES.	DEFINITIONS OF DERIVATIVES.
In *in; not.*	**trude** *thrust.*	**In trude',**	*thrust in; encroach.*
Ig *in; not.*	**nore** *know.*	**Ig nore,**	*not to know; not to recognize.*
Il *in; not.*	**lume** *light.*	**Il lume,**	*throw light in, or on.*
Im *in; not.*	**merge** *plunge.*	**Im merge,**	*plunge in; immerse.*
Ir *in; not.*	**radiate** *shine.*	**Ir ra' di ate,**	*shine in upon; illume.*
Inter *between.*	**lay** *put.*	**In ter lay',**	*lay or put between.*
Enter *between.*	**prise** *take.*	**En' ter prise,**	*take between hands; undertake.*

EXERCISE 444.

Forms of EX and ANTI.

PREFIXES.	RADICALS.	DERIVATIVES.	DEFINITIONS OF DERIVATIVES.
Ex *out.*	**pand** *spread.*	**Ex pand',**	*spread out; enlarge.*
Ec *out.*	**centric** *central.*	**Ec cen' tric,**	*out of the centre; odd.*
Ef *out.*	**fulge** *shine.*	**Ef fulge',**	*shine out; beam.*
E *out.*	**volve** *roll.*	**E volve,**	*roll out; develop.*
Anti *against.*	**dote** *given.*	**An' ti dote,**	*what is given against poison.*
Ant *against.*	**acid** *sour.*	**Ant ac' id,**	*remedy against acid.*

EXERCISE 445.

Forms of AB and CONTRA.

PREFIXES.	RADICALS.	DERIVATIVES.	DEFINITIONS OF DERIVATIVES.
Ab *from.*	**solve** *loose.*	**Ab solve',**	*loose, or free from.*
Abs *from.*	**tain** *hold.*	**Ab stain,**	*hold, or keep from.*
A *from.*	**move** *stir.*	**A move,**	*to stir, or move from.*
Contra *against.*	**dict** *speak.*	**Con tra dict',**	*speak against; deny.*
Contro *against.*	**vert** *turn.*	**Con tro vert,**	*turn against; contest.*
Counter *against.*	**poise** *weigh.*	**Coun ter poise,**	*weigh against; to equal in weight.*

EXERCISE 446.

Forms of DIS, SUPER AND SYN.

PREFIXES.	RADICALS.	DERIVATIVES.	DEFINITIONS OF DERIVATIVES.
Dis *apart.*	**tend** *stretch.*	**Dis tend',**	*stretch apart, or out.*
Dif *apart.*	**fract** *break.*	**Dif fract,**	*break apart, or in pieces.*
Di *apart.*	**verge** *bend.*	**Di verge,**	*bend, or tend apart; vary.*
Super *over.*	**vene** *come.*	**Su per vene',**	*come over, or upon; happen.*
Sur *over.*	**pass** *step.*	**Sur pass,**	*step over; excel.*
Syn *together.*	**opsis** *view.*	**Syn op sis,**	*view together; general view.*
Syl *together.*	**lable** *a taking.*	**Syl' la ble.**	*a taking together of letters, so as to form one sound.*
Sym *together.*	**posium** *a drinking.*	**Sym po' si um,**	*a drinking together; feast.*

SECTION XXI.

SUFFIXES.

In this Section, the Radicals, being for the most part, very simple, are left without *separate* definition. In the first column, therefore, will be found the SUFFIXES, in the second, the DEFINITIONS OF THE SUFFIXES, in the third, the DERIVATIVES, and in the fourth, the DEFINITIONS OF THE DERIVATIVES.

EXERCISE 447.

SUFFIXES.	DEFINITIONS.	DERIVATIVES.	DEFINITIONS OF DERIVATIVES.
ate*	*to make.*	Lu' bric ate,	*to make* lubric or slippery.
ate	*made like.*	Glob ate,	*made like* a globe.
en	*to make.*	Soft en,	*to make* soft.
en	*made of.*	Silk en,	*made of* silk.
fy	*to make.*	Rar e fy,	*to make* rare, or thin.
ify	*to make.*	Just i fy,	*to make or prove* just.
ize	*to make.*	Civ il ize,	*to make* civil.
ing	*continuing to.*	Walk ing,	*continuing* to walk.
ed	*did.*	Mark ed,	*did* mark.
ed	*having.*	Skill ed,	*having* skill.
ar	*one who.*	Beg gar,	*one who* begs.
er	*one who.*	Pay er,	*one who* pays.
ee	*one who.*	Pay ee',	*one who* receives pay.
or	*one who.*	Act' or,	*one who* acts.
an	*one who.*	Ro' man,	*one who* is a native of Rome.
ate	*one who.*	Cu rate,	*one who* has a cure; a pastor.
ist	*one who.*	Art ist,	*one who* is skilled in art.

* ATE and EN, in common with FY, IFY, and IZE, are defined above by the phrase "*to make*;" because they are commonly used to form verbs. This phrase, "*to make*," is taken, as a definition, merely for the sake of convenience. In many cases, other definitions, as "*to cause*," "*to put*," &c., will be found more suitable. Sometimes the suffix is the mere *sign* of a verb; as loc*ate*, *to place*.

Besides this use, however, ATE and EN, as is seen in the text, to which may be added the suffix ED, are employed to form participles and participial adjectives; and, are then defined by such phrases as, "*made of*," "*made into*," "*made*, or *formed like*," "*having*," "*affected by*," &c.

EXERCISE 448.

SUFFIXES.	DEFINITIONS.	DERIVATIVES.	DEFINITIONS OF DERIVATIVES.
ner	*one who.*	**Part′ ner,**	*one who* has or owns a part.
ster	*one who.*	**Team ster,**	*one who* drives a team.
yer	*one who.*	**Law yer,**	*one who* is versed in law.
isan	*one who.*	**Par ti san,**	*one who* sides with a party.
zen	*one who.*	**Cit i zen,**	*one who* dwells in a city.
ess	*a female.*	**Li on ess,**	*a female* of the lion tribe.
ine	*a female.*	**Her o ine,**	a heroic *female.*
ix	*a female.*	**Me di a′ trix,**	*a female* that mediates.

EXERCISE 449.

ity*	*quality, or state of being.*	**Pub lic′ i ty,**	*quality or state of being* public.
cy		**Pri′ va cy,**	*quality or state of being* private.
ancy		**Oc cu pan cy,**	*quality or state of being* occupied.
ance		**Vig il ance,**	*state of being* vigilant.
ency		**Tend en cy,**	*quality or state of* tending.
ence		**Ad her′ ence,**	*quality or state of* adhering.
ude		**Qui′ et ude,**	*state of being* quiet.
ness		**Rude ness,**	*quality of being* rude.
ion	*the act of; that which.*	**Mo tion,**	*act of* moving.
ment		**Move ment,**	*act of* moving.
ure		**Seiz ure,**	*act of* seizing.

EXERCISE 450.

al	*pertaining or relating to.*	**Fa′ tal,**	*pertaining to* fate.
ern		**East ern,**	*relating to* the East.
ic		**He ro′ ic,**	*pertaining to* a hero.
an		**Af′ ri can,**	*pertaining to* Africa.
ine		**Ser pen tine,**	*pertaining to* a serpent.
ile		**In fant ile,**	*pertaining to* an infant.
ar		**Con sul ar,**	*relating to* a consul.
ary		**Com et a ry,**	*relating to* a comet.
ical		**Po et′ ic al,**	*relating to* a poet.

EXERCISE 451.

ous†	*full of; of the nature of.*	**Dan′ ger ous,**	*full of* danger.
ose		**Ver bose′,**	*full of* words.
ful‡		**Hope′ ful,**	*full of* hope.
y		**Jui cy,**	*full of* juice.
ey		**Clay ey,**	*of the nature of* clay.
ly	*in a—manner.*	**Rude ly,**	*in a* rude *manner.*
able	*that may or can be; fit to be.*	**Trace a ble,**	*that may be* traced.
ible		**Ed i ble,**	*fit to be* eaten.
ific	*producing.*	**Tor por if′ ic,**	*producing* torpor.
ics	*the science of.*	**Op tics,**	*the science of* vision.

* This Suffix has two other forms, ETY and TY; as, in vari*ety*, and novel*ty*.

† The Suffix OUS has several forms, as EOUS, CEOUS, etc.

‡ The Suffix FUL, when, with a radical, it forms a noun, signifies "*what, or as much as, will fill;*" as, hand*ful, what,* or *as much as, will fill* the hand; arm*ful, what will fill* the arm.

EXERCISE 452.

SUFFIXES.	DEFINITIONS.	DERIVATIVES.	DEFINITIONS OF DERIVATIVES.
age*	*the act of.*	Cart' age,	*the act of* carting.
oid	*having the form.*	Sphe roid,	*having the form of* a sphere.
er	*more.*	Hard er,	*more* hard.
est	*most.*	Hard est,	*most* hard.
esce	*to grow.*	Co a lesce',	*to grow* together; unite.
escent	*becoming.*	A ces' cent,	*becoming* sour.
escence	*act of becoming.*	A ces cence,	*act of becoming* sour.
ism†	*doctrine.*	Mor' mon ism,	*the doctrine of* the Mormons.
less	*without.*	Cash less,	*without* cash.
ish	*somewhat.*	New ish,	*somewhat* new.
some	*somewhat.*	Lone some,	*somewhat* lonely.

EXERCISE 453.

ship		Lord' ship,	*the rank of* a lord.
hood	*rank, office, state,*	Child hood,	*the state of being* a child.
ric	*or jurisdiction of.*	Bish op ric,	*the jurisdiction of* a Bishop.
dom		Pope dom,	*the jurisdiction of* the Pope.
y‡		Glut ton y,	*the practice of* a glutton.
ry	*the art or prac-*	Big ot ry,	*the practice of* a bigot.
ary	*tice of; or the*	Stat u a ry,	*the art of* making statues.
ery	*place where.*	Cook er y,	*the art of* cooking.
ory		Arm or y,	*place where* arms are kept.
ward	*toward.*	West ward,	*toward* the West.

EXERCISE 454.

ive	*tending to, or hav-*	Pre vent' ive,	*tending to* prevent.
ory	*ing the nature of.*	Ex' pi a to ry,	*tending to* expiate.
kin		Lamb kin,	a *little* lamb.
ling		Gos ling,	a *little*, or *young* goose.
cule		An i mal' cule,	a *minute* animal.
ule		Glob' ule,	a *little* globe.
cle	*little, petty, or*	Tu ber cle,	a *little* tumor.
icle	*minute.*	Par ti cle,	a *minute* part.
ock		Hill ock,	a *little* hill.
et		Flow er et,	a *little* flower.
let		Ring let,	a *little* ring, or curl
aster		Po et as ter,	a *petty* poet.

* The Suffix AGE, signifies, also, *the cost of, the place where*, the *rank* or *condition*, as also an *assemblage* of things.

† This Suffix deserves special notice. It marks *what is peculiar to* persons or things; and hence denotes a *doctrine* or *system*, *a state* or *condition*, as also *an idiom* in language.

‡ Y, RY, ARY, ERY, ORY, are merely different forms of the same prefix. Beside the meanings given above, they often denote a body or number of things taken *collectively;* as, perfum*ery*, a collection of perfumes yeoman*ry*, the body or mass of yeomen.

SECTION XXII.

ANALYSIS OF COMPOUND WORDS.

Here, in the first and second columns, the parts of each compound are separately given, with the definitions *underneath*. In the third column, they are brought together again, and, in the fourth, defined as one word.

EXERCISE 455.

FIRST PART.	SECOND PART.	COMPOUNDS.	DEFINITIONS.
Homi, *man.*	**cide,** *a killing.*	**Hom' i cide,**	the killing of a man.
Parri, *parent.*		**Par' ri cide,**	the killing of a parent.
Infanti, *infant.*		**In fant' i cide,**	the killing of an infant.
Matri, *mother.*		**Mat' ri cide,**	the killing of a mother.
Fratri, *brother.*		**Frat' ri cide,**	the killing of a brother.
Regi, *king.*		**Reg' i cide,**	the killing of a king.
Sui, *self.*		**Su' i cide,**	the killing of one's self.

EXERCISE 456.

FIRST PART.	SECOND PART.	COMPOUNDS.	DEFINITIONS.
Demo, *people.*	**oracy,** *rule.*	**De moc' ra cy,**	rule of the people.
Aristo, *noble.*		**Ar is toc' ra cy**	rule of the nobles.
Ortho, *right.*	**dox,** *doctrine.*	**Or' tho dox,**	right in doctrine.
Hetero, *other.*		**Het' e ro dox,**	other, or different in doctrine.
Hippo, *horse.*	**drome,** *course.*	**Hip' po drome,**	horse-course; race-course.
Aque, *water.*	**duct,** *channel.*	**Aq' ue duct,**	channel for water.
Agri, *field.*	**culture,** *tillage.*	**Ag' ri cul ture,**	tillage of fields; farming.
Horti, *garden.*		**Hor' ti cul ture,**	culture of a garden; gardening.

EXERCISE 457.

FIRST PART.	SECOND PART.	COMPOUNDS.	DEFINITIONS.
Tri, *three.*	ennial, *year, or yearly.*	**Tri en' ni al,**	once in three years.
Cent, *hundred.*		**Cen ten' ni al,**	once in a hundred years.
Mill, *thousand.*		**Mil len' ni al,**	pertaining to a thousand years.
Fructi, *fruit.*	ferous, *bearing.*	**Fruc tif' er ous,**	bearing, or producing fruit.
Flori, *flower.*		**Flo rif' er ous,**	bearing, or producing flowers.
Denti, *tooth.*	frice, *rubbing.*	**Dent' i frice,**	preparation to rub or clean the teeth.
Cruci, *cross.*	form, *shape.*	**Cru' ci form,**	having the form of a cross.
Ovi, *egg.*		**O' vi form,**	having the form of an egg.

EXERCISE 458.

FIRST PART.	SECOND PART.	COMPOUNDS.	DEFINITIONS.
Melli, *honey.*	fluous, *flowing.*	**Mel lif' lu ous,**	flowing with honey; sweet.
Felli, *gall.*		**Fel lif' lu ous,**	flowing with gall; bitter.
Igni, *fire.*		**Ig nif' lu ous,**	flowing with fire.
Octa, *eight.*	hedron, *side.*	**Oc ta he' dron,**	figure having eight sides.
Poly, *many.*		**Pol y he dron,**	figure having many sides.
Febri, *fever.*	fuge, *a chasing away.*	**Feb' ri fuge,**	that which chases away or subdues fever.
Vermi, *worm.*		**Verm' i fuge,**	that which chases away or expels worms.

EXERCISE 459.

FIRST PART.	SECOND PART.	COMPOUNDS.	DEFINITIONS.
Hexa, *six.*	gon, *angle.*	**Hex' a gon,**	a figure having six angles.
Octa, *eight.*		**Oc' ta gon,**	a figure having eight angles.
Poly, *many.*		**Pol' y gon,**	a figure having many angles.
Poly, *many.*	glot, *tongue.*	**Pol' y glot,**	containing many tongues.
Homo, *same.*	geneous, *having the nature.*	**Ho mo ge' ne ous,**	having the same nature.
Hetero, *other.*		**Het e ro ge' ne ous,**	having a different nature.

EXERCISE 460.

FIRST PART.	SECOND PART.	COMPOUNDS.	DEFINITIONS.
Belli, *war.*	**gerous,** *bearing.*	**Bel lig′ er ous,**	bearing, or bringing war.
Crini, *hair.*		**Cri nig′ er ous,**	bearing, or having hair.
Lani, *wool.*		**La nig′ er ous,**	bearing, or having wool.
Auto, *self.*	**graph,** *writing.*	**Au′ to graph,**	the hand-writing of one's self.
Tele, *far off.*		**Tel′ e graph,**	contrivance for writing from afar.
Magni, *large.*	**loquence,** *talk.*	**Mag nil′ o quence,**	big talk; pompous language.
Grandi, *grand.*		**Gran dil′ o quence,**	great talk; lofty speaking.

EXERCISE 461.

FIRST PART.	SECOND PART.	COMPOUNDS.	DEFINITIONS.
Bio, *life.*	**graphy,** *a writing; marking; description.*	**Bi og′ ra phy,**	a writing, or history of one's self.
Steno, *short.*		**Ste nog′ ra phy,**	short-hand writing.
Typo, *type.*		**Ty pog′ ra phy,**	a marking with types; printing.
Topo, *place.*		**To pog′ ra phy,**	a description of places.
Geo, *earth.*		**Ge og′ ra phy,**	a description of the earth.
Ortho, *right,*		**Or thog′ ra phy,**	correct writing; spelling.

EXERCISE 462.

FIRST PART.	SECOND PART.	COMPOUNDS.	DEFINITIONS.
Geo, *earth.*	**logy,** *word; reason; science.*	**Ge ol′ o gy,**	science of the formation of the earth.
Zoo, *animal.*		**Zo ol′ o gy,**	science of animals.
Theo, *God.*		**The ol′ o gy,**	the science which treats of God.
Concho, *shell.*		**Conch ol′ o gy,**	science of shells.
Chrono, *time.*		**Chro nol′ o gy,**	science of computing time or dates.
Cyclo, *circle.*	**pedia,** *knowledge; science.*	**Cy clo pe′ di a,**	circle of the arts and sciences.
Hydro, *water.*	**phobia,** *dread.*	**Hy dro pho′ bi a,**	dread of water; canine madness.
Hippo, *horse.*	**potamus,** *river.*	**Hip po pot′ a mus,**	a river-horse.

EXERCISE 463.

FIRST PART.	SECOND PART.	COMPOUNDS.	DEFINITIONS.
Cosmo, *world.*	**polite,** *citizen.*	**Cos mop' o lite,**	a citizen of the world.
Aero, *air.*	**naut,** *one who sails.*	**A' er o naut,**	one who sails in or navigates the air.
Poly, *many.*	**nesia,** *islands.*	**Pol y ne' sia,**	consisting of many islands.
Tri, *three.*	**nomial** *a name; a term.*	**Tri no' mi al,**	consisting of three terms or members.
Quadri, *four.*		**Quad ri no' mi al,**	consisting of four terms or members.
Poly, *many.*		**Pol y no' mi al,**	consisting of many terms or members.

EXERCISE 464.

Astro, *star.*	**nomy,** *law.*	**As tron' o my,**	law, or science of the stars.
Eco, *house.*		**E con' o my,**	law, or rule of a house; thriftiness.
Deutero, *second.*		**Deu ter on' o my,**	second law, or fifth book of Moses.
Pan, *all.*	**orama,** *view.*	**Pan o ra' ma,**	a complete view; view of all.
Cosm, *world.*		**Cos mo ra' ma,**	view of the world.
Tele *far off.*	**scope,** *a view or sight.*	**Tel' e scope,**	instrument to view things far off.
Micro, *small.*		**Mi' cro scope,**	instrument to view things minute.

EXERCISE 465.

Philo, *love.*	**sophy,** *wisdom.*	**Phi los' o phy,**	love of wisdom; knowledge.
Penta, *five.*	**teuch,** *book.*	**Pen' ta teuch,**	the five books of Moses.
Pyro, *fire.*	**technic,** *relating to art.*	**Py ro tech' nic,**	relating to the art of making fire-works.
Poly, *many.*		**Pol y tech' nic,**	relating to many arts.
Stereo, *solid.*	**type,** *mark; emblem.*	**Ste' re o type,**	solid type; plate of metallic type.
Carni, *flesh.*	**vorous,** *eating, or devouring.*	**Car niv' o rous,**	flesh-eating, or devouring.
Grani, *grain.*		**Gra niv' o rous,**	grain-eating, or devouring.*

* For a course of study in the analysis of Derivatives and Compounds exclusively, see Sanders & McElligott's ANALYSIS OF ENGLISH WORDS.

SECTION XXIII.

TEST WORDS.

To bring under special review what has been taught in the previous part of this book, and to *test*, by pertinent examples, the pupil's proficiency in the art of spelling generally, is the leading aim of the present Section.

In aid of this design, notes are not unfrequently subjoined, pointing the learner back to the page or exercise, where may be found the rule, exception, principle, or what not, involved in the spelling or pronunciation of the particular word before him.

Other notes, also, are added, embracing points not elsewhere introduced, or such as seemed to require some additional explanation.

The examples, moreover, are often so arranged as almost to *compel* comparison between such words and parts of words as *British* (*one t*) and *skittish* (*two t's*), *distaff* (*ff*) and *digraph* (*ph*), *typify* (*ify*) and *tepefy* (*efy*), which are among the most fertile sources of error in orthography.

EXERCISE 466.

ab' scess
căis' son
ba' sin
răi' sin
dis' taff
di' graph
hâre' lip
jack' al
măel' strom
num' skull
ôr' ġiēs
right' eous
sib' yl
tôr' toise (-*tis*)
wind' row
shack' les
mis spell'

cat' e chism
dis' ci pline
dis' si pate
ep' au let
et i quette' (-*ket*)
fi' e ry
wīr' y
gel' a tine
guil' lo tine
maġ' is trate
maj' es ty
mol' li fy
os' si fy
paç' i fy
liq' ua ble
liq' ui date
măr' i gold

a poc' ry phă
a pos' ta sy
ar is toc' ra cy
ab o li' tion
eb ul li' tion
phi los' o phy
phy lac' ter y
rhī noç' e ros
e vis' cer ate
com miș' er ate
syn on' y mous
tris' yl la ble
fe roç' i ty
ver bos' i ty
phthis' ick y*
ap pa ri' tion
cat e chu' men

* In forming *phthisicky* from *phthisic*, why is the *k* inserted? See Rule VI, page 61.

EXERCISE 467.

ber′ yl	ben′ i ṣon	a e′ ri al†
fer′ rule (*ril*)	em blā′ *zon*	fu ne′ re al†
cam′ phor	de pend′ ence	bo tan′ ic al†
sul′ phur	at tend′ ance	tȳ ran′ nic al
dou*b*t′ ing*	fal′ la cy	cha me′ le on
dough′ ty	pol′ i cy	crī te′ ri on
elf′ in	fan′ ta sy	ca̤u′ li flow er
da̤u′ phin	hol′ ly hock	gil′ li flow er
e clă*t*′	hol′ o ca̤ust	neç′ es sa ry
hu̇z zä′	hor′ ri fy	ne ces′ si ty
lat′ tice	tor′ re fy	ter ra′ que ous†
let′ tuce (-*tis*)	man da rĭn′	ob se′ qui ous
tēa′ ṣ*e*lṣ	pis ta reen′	po li an′ thēṣ
mēa′ ṣl*e*ṣ	baṣ′ i lisk	pol y an′ thus
wēa′ ṣ*e*lṣ	ob′ e lisk	diph the′ ri ȧ

EXERCISE 468.

for′ age	pen′ ni less	so lil′ o quy†
por′ ridge	pen′ ny weight	col′ lo quy
sca lene′	pĭ o neer′	syl′ lo giṣm
tu reen′	cav a liēr′	ven tril′ o quiṣm
ter rene′	côurt′ e sy	cem′ e ter y
ton tïne′	côurte′ sy	sym′ me try†
fag′ ot	in fring′ ing‡	far i na′ ceous
mag′ got	singe′ ing	con sci en′ tious
mi räge′ (-*räzh′*)	twinge′ ing	col liṣ′ ion
pip′ pin	an′ nu al	co a li′ tion
nas′ cent	man′ u al	su per sti′ tious
piqu′ ant	ap ro pōṣ′	dī aph′ a nous
tan′ ṣy	viġ′ i lance	em pȳr′ e al
co′ zy	prev′ a lence	em pĭr′ ic al
de bris′ (*dā bree′*)	com′ plai ṣance	pal′ at a ble
	cog′ ni zance	gar ru̇′ li ty

* Why is *b* silent in *doubting?* See Assimilation of Consonants, p. 13.

† For the accent on these words, see pages 78 and 79.

‡ Why is the *e* omitted in *infringing*, and retained in *singeing* and *twingeing?* See note, page 68.

EXERCISE 469.

jal′ ap	ras call′ ion	mac a ro′ nĭ
scạl′ lop	bat tal′ ion	maeh i na′ tion
trol′ lop	bi′ as *e*d	re cep′ ta cle
wạl′ lop	com′ pass *e*d	el lip′ tic al
wạd′ y	buc ca neer′	san′ a to ry*
shod′ dy	brig a diēr′	san′ i ta ry
with ạl′	căr′ ri on	plan′ et a ry
fore stạll′	clăr′ i on	er ro′ ne ous
zouäve (*zwäv*)	cel′ er y	sym pho′ ni ous
yạ*ch*t′ ing	cel′ lar age	au toc′ ra cy
prāi′ rie	ser′ aph ïne	hy poc′ ri sy
dāi′ ry	cam′ phene	vī ca′ ri ous
di′ a ry	cop′ per as	cal ca′ re ous
fri′ ar	cop′ y right	ac ces′ sa ry*
bri′ er	crit′ i cişm	ac ces′ so ry
tôr′ sion	wit′ ti cişm	căr′ i ca ture
tẽr′ tian	veġ′ e tate	chăr′ ac ter ize

EXERCISE 470.

wạltz′ ing	de poş′ it	com′ mis sa ry
wheel′ *w*right	com poş′ ite	em′ is sa ry
ko′ ran	fal la′ cious	e ma′ ci ate
eho′ ral	her ba′ ceous	ex pa′ ti ate
breez′ y	frip′ per y	mon stros′ i ty
cheeş′ y	dra′ per y	reç i proç′ i ty
lam′ pass	gāy′ e ty	no vi′ ti ate
gram′ pus	la′ i ty	ex crụ′ ci ate
browse	hạl′ i but	vae çi na′ tion
grouse	hol′ o graph	vaç il la′ tion
ban′ yan	id′ i om	tel lu′ ri an
ūn′ ion	vac′ u um	va le′ ri an
aē′ rie	in sẽr′ tion	sal e ra′ tus
*b*dell′ ium	in vẽr′ sion	in iq′ ui tous
chil′ blāin	tran scend′ ent†	buş′ y bod y‡
se pạwn′	as cend′ ant†	an′ y where‡

* *Sanatory, conducing to* health, as sanatory measures; *sanitary, pertaining to* health; *accessary,* aiding in crime; *accessory,* additional.

† For a note on words of this class, see page 86.

‡ What sound has *u* in *busybody,* and *a* in *anywhere?* See page 37.

EXERCISE 471.

stir′ rup	ver mil′ ion	ab o riġ′ i nēs̠
poi*g*n′ ant	quin till′ ion	ad mis′ si ble
phy s̠ïque′	ter′ ri fy	ad mit′ ta ble*
mur′ raïn	ver′ i fy	mis tāk′ a ble
*k*nap′ sack	tu′ me fy	ad vēr′ tïs̠e ment
gam′ ut	typ′ i fy	bac ca lau′ re ate
cum′ in	tep′ e fy	bac cha na′ li an
vēr′ min	traġ′ e dy	cat e chet′ ic al
salt′-r*h*eum	tal′ is̠ mans̠	da guerre′ o type
särce′ net	am′ ber grïs	da guerre′ i an
côrse′ let	a cous′ tics	ir rev′ er ence
boûr ġeois′ (*-jois*)	băr ri cade′	per se vēr′ ance
bou quet′ (*-ka′*)	băr′ y tone	Ec cle s̠i as′ tēs̠
swap′ ping	ba nä′ na	e van gel′ ic al
thwack′ ing	ban dan′ a	e ques′ tri an

EXERCISE 472.

ches*t*′ nut	bär′ be cūe	chi rop′ o dist
a bys̠m′	can′ ni bal	ex̠ aġ′ ġer ate
war′ rant	cel′ an dine	hi′ e rarch y
Wednes̠′ day (*wĕnz dy*)	chlo′ ro form	hȳ dro pho′ bi a
awn′ ing	chant′ i cleer	hȳ per crit′ ic al
blows̠e	chrys′ a lis	hyp o crit′ ic al
boo′ s̠y	chrys′ o lite	id i o syn′ cra sy
ooz′ y	Cy re′ ne	mel lif′ er ous
bōwl′ ing	dal′ li ance	in tel′ li gi ble
trōll′ ing	de scen′ sion	i ras′ ci ble
çham′ ois (*-my*)	dis sen′ sion	Lil i pu′ tian
ba rege′ (*-rāj*)	dis pēr′ sive	man′ tua-māk er
chim′ neys	dis cûr′ sive	mil len′ ni um
cher′ ries†	eū′ cha rist	vi cis′ si tude
	ex̠ em′ plar	mus co va′ do

* See Exercise 281, page 86. Note that adjectives formed from *English* words by suffixing *able* or *ible*, as *readable* from *read*, commonly prefer the form *able*. Those from Latin end in *able* or *ible*, according as they end in *abilis* or *ibilis* in that language.

† Why, in the plural of *cherry* (*cherries*), is *y* changed into *i*, and not in *chimneys*? See Rules XII and XIII, pages 69 and 70.

EXERCISE 473.

quay′ age (*kē-*)
hey′ day
ga′ la-day*
liq′ uor
lac′ *qu*er
mis spend′
neigh′ bor
ped′ dler
pam′ phlet
phal′ anx
piēce′ meal
*p*shaw
*p*seū′ do
pust′ ule
qua′ haug

de mûr′ rer
fal′ li ble
fa tĭgu′ ing
fric as seed′
*gh*ȧst′ li ness
gos′ sa mer
ġĭr′ an dole
han*d*′ ker chief
ho ri′ zon
hŏr′ o loġe
Hu′ ḡ*u*e not
hur′ ri cane
ich neū′ mon
i′ ron y
im promp′ tu

Ne a pol′ i tan
ef face′ a ble†
pûr′ chăs a ble
os ten′ si ble
pet′ ti fog ḡer
pi ä′ no-fōr te
phys i og′ no my
pre sent′ i ment
pre sent′ ment
pet ri fac′ tion
pu tre fac′ tion
re cog′ nĭ zance
re con′ noĭs sänce
rem i nis′ cence
sep a ra′ tion

EXERCISE 474.

rac coon′
rey′ nard
whim′ sey
cup′ board‡
clap′ bōard
sc*h*ism
scrive′ ner
sou ve nir′
sôr′ g*h*um
tis′ sue (*-shu*)
tou′ can
trāipse
tran scribe′
tres′ *t*le
twad′ dle

i′ sin glȧss
kan ga roo′
ka′ ty did
log′ a rithms
mag a zïne′
hy′ gi ene
man′ i kin
me dall′ ion
man dil′ ion
o paque′ ness
piqu′ an cy
ple′ ia dēs
pleū′ ri sy
pol′ li wig
pol′ y chord

su per sēd′ ure
thór′ ōugh wort
u biq′ ui ty
lo quaç′ i ty
ver i sim′ i lar
*w*hōōp′ ing-cough
ab er ra′ tion
a ceph′ a lous
a′ er a ted
al to ḡeth′ er
an ni vêr′ sa ry
av oĭr du pois′
bel liġ′ er ent
as sas′ sin ate
brag ga do′ ci o

* What is the general Rule for the insertion of the hyphen in compound words? See note, page 75. What, for accenting them? See page 80.

† Why, in forming *effaceable* from *efface*, is not the final *e* in the latter dropped? See Exercise 224, and the second note on page 68.

‡ On the sound of *p*, in the words *cupboard* and *clapboard*, see page 9.

EXERCISE 475.

cac′ tus
cap′ stan
cor′ al
crev′ ice
de tach′
un latch′
diph′ thong
dōugh′ nut
ȩight′ een
flac′ çid
gâir′ ish
gāug′ ing
goug′ ing
*g*na̤w′ ing
heärk′ *en*

pa vil′ ion
no nill′ ion
punc til′ ious
pel′ i can
re lig′ ious
ren′ dez vous
(*rĕn′ de voo*)
re′ qui em
de ten′ tion
ex ten′ sion
sa̤lt′-cel lar
sat′ el lite
scûr′ ril ous
shib′ bo leth
sib′ yl līne

ef fer ves′ cence
el ee mos′ y na ry
e mol′ li ent
ex hil′ a rate
fa̤l′ si fi er
fôr′ ti fy ing
hyp o chon′ dri ac
math e ma ti′ cian
mis′ cel la ny
o rang′-o̤u tang′
par a pher na′li à
pla′ gi a rism
port man′ teau (*to*)
spẽrm a ce′ ti
tax′ i der mist

EXERCISE 476.

hym′ ning
mär′ tyr
meer′ sçha̤um
mes′ sieurs
(*mesh′ yerz*)
nan keen′
nick′ el
pal′ lor
pärs′ ley
pic′ nic
pīc′ bald
plagu′ y
pôr′ poise (*pus*)

syc′ a more
tan′ ner y
ti a′ rà
ter′ ra pin
ter′ a phim
tam bo̤ur ïne′
com mit′ ted
com mu′ ted
tre men′ dous
vac′ çi nate
val′ or ous
den′ i zen
ven′ i ṣon

up hōl′ ster y
an tiq′ ui ty
ap pel la′ tion
ap pûr′ te nance
bo′ a-con strict′ or
can cel la′ tion*
cas′ tel la ted
cap′ il la ry
colonel′ cy
(*kur′ nel sy*)
ka leī′ do scope
er y sip′ e las
Feb′ ru a ry

* *Cancellation*, if formed from *cancel*, by adding the suffix *ation*, might pass for an exception to Rule VIII, page 63, and be set down among the list of exceptions, like *crystalline*, *metallic*, etc., as in Exercise 210. But, in *reality*, none of this class of words form exceptions to the rule, if we consider that in the languages whence they come to us (Latin, through the French and the Greek), the *l* is doubled already. But for the *merely* English scholar, they *are* exceptions, and for convenience, may be so treated.

EXERCISE 477.

re hëarse′	vit′ re ous	ha bil′ i ment
*rh*om′ boid	vit′ ri ol	in no va′ tion
rọuge (*roozh*)	whif′ fle tree	mel′ an ehol y
sçhnapps	o bẹi′ sance	ob liq′ ui ty
sçhot′ tish }	a bẹy′ ance	ob′ lo quy
sçhot′ tisçhe }	al′ ba tross	pe tro′ le um
Brit′ ish	Ma lac′ ca	pri mo ge′ ni al
skit′ tish	al pac′ à	ho mo ge′ ne al
squïrm	ạl be′ it	rec on noi′ ter
stärve′ ling	as cer tāin′	re ṣist i′ ble
suc çinct′	bach′ e lor	*rh*et o ri′ cian
suf fice′ (*fize*)	be lēa′ *gu*er	scin til la′ tion
swarth′ y	bob′ o link	tee to′ tal er
tọn′ nage	bụl′ le tin	syl lab i ca′ tion
trom′ bone	cas′ si mere	Chat ta noo′ gȧ
vel′ lum	cat a falque′	sa lu′ ta to ry
whiz′ zing	coch′ i neal	sus cep′ ti ble

EXERCISE 478.

a g*h*äst′	cȯl′ an der	pu sil lan′ i mous
ban′ tam	cŏl on nade′	pol′ y the iṣm
bụd′ d*h*iṣm	col′ o nize	re frig′ er a tor
chăl′ dron	deç′ i mal	re ju′ ve nate
cạl′ dron	dĕr′ e lict	re tal′ i ate
cọu′ gar	des *h*à bille′	pal′ li ate
cọu′ pon (*pong*)	di′ a mond	vi tres′ ci ble
cär′ cass	E gyp′ tian	ac cess′ i ble
co lo*g*ne′	em băr′ rass	re miss′ i ble
de bu*t*′	ex cres′ cence	ac qui es′ cence
cụsh′ ion	reç′ i pe*	a nal′ o gous
ēk′ ing	frol′ ic some	as păr′ a gus
gäp′ ing	rol′ lick ing	a nom′ a lous
eph′ od	guer ril′ là	cat′ e go ry
a thwạrt′	gy ra′ tion	cor′ ri gi ble
cŏn′ duït	hand′ i work	cor rupt′ i ble
con tọur′	hẹin′ ous ness	di e tet′ ies

* For a note on *e* final, on such words as *recipe*, see page 39.

EXERCISE 479.

bāil′ iff
ca′ liph
ehyle
ehyme
Christ′ mas
cor tege′ (tāzh′)
dis pâir′
eū′ ehre*
fledġe′ ling
front′ iēr
gnash′ ing
grand′ eūr
dan′ druff
horn′ blende
van dyke′
Il′ i ad
im′ be cïle
in vēi′ gle
aids-de-camp†
(ăds-de-kŏng)
laç′ er ate
lull′ a by̆
mac′ ca boy
ma çhïn′ ist
man′ di ble
me rï′ no
năr′ ra tive
bal za rïne′
ob nox′ ious
om′ e let
et y mol′ o gy
ex traôr′ di na ry
flaġ el la′ tion
her cu′ le an
in tel′ li gence
men ag′ e rie
(men ăzh′ e re)
neū ral′ gi ȧ
o po del′ doc
par e gor′ ic
per en′ ni al
per tur ba′ tion
pol′ y syl la ble
su per fï′ ciēs
tap i o′ cȧ

EXERCISE 480.

hour′ ī
flow′ er y
jäun′ dice
kĕel′ son
elïque
cȯm′ frey
blanc-mange′
(blo monj′)
dac′ tyl
dew′ y
duc′ at
en fĕoff′
en nui′
(ong nwē′)
flam′ beau (bo)
o pos′ sum
păr′ a çhute
par′ a ly̆ze
par′ o quet
phar′ i see
ret′ i cence
rhap′ so dy
sab′ a oth
sas′ sa fras
sçin′ til late
ven′ ti late
Sçyth′ i an
si roc′ cōs‡
stadt′ hōld er
Teū ton′ ic
waf′ fle-i ron
Ab ys sin′ i an
am phib′ i ous
a poc′ a lypse
ap pa ra′ tus
ar ehi pel′ a go
ce lib′ a cy
ben e fï′ ci a ry
con stel la′ tion
de te′ ri o rate
el′ i gi ble
gut′ tȧ-pēr′ chȧ
ir ri ga′ tion
mam ma′ li ȧ
mĕr′ ry-an′ drew

* On words ending like *euchre*, see note, page 87.

† In re-spelling words from the French, we employ the combination *ng* (as in *ăd-de-kong*), merely to indicate the *nasal* sound heard in pronouncing the syllables, *an*, *en*, *on*, etc., in that language.

‡ On the spelling of the plurals of words ending in *o*, see note, page 73.

EXERCISE 481.

gam boge'	tom' a hawk	met ro pol' i tan
găr rote'	trĕas' ur er	nul li fi ca' tion
go' pher	trou' ba dour	o ver-bal' ance
gran' ĭte	vas' sal age	pan e gўr' ic
haws' er	mu' ci lage	pär' ti cĭ ple
*k*nick' *k*nacks	vĕr' di gris	pe riph' e ry
mem' ior (*wôr*)	zo' o phўte	phi lol' o gy
môr' phĭne	am a teur'	*p*neū mo' ni a
mush' room	im ma tūre'	rep a ra' tion
mulct	con noĭs seur'	sar sa pa ril' lȧ
myth	am' e thyst	tes' sel la ted
pæ' an	an' te pȧst	ter res' tri al
pe lïsse'	an' ti tўpe	u til i ta' ri an
pen' guin	Ap' en nīnes	ac com' pa ni ment
san' guine	av a lançhe'	al lege' a ble
phos' phor	bron chī' tis	a er o stat' ics

EXERCISE 482.

plum*b*' ing	buoy' an cy*	Ap pa la' chi an
quartz	poi*g*n' an cy	ap prox' i mate
quï vïve' (*ke vēv'*)	cat' a cōm*b*s	a rith me tĭ' cian
rāi' ment	ci vil' ian	con fec' tion er y
re scind'	oc till' ion	con va les' cent
ro sette'	be numb' *ed*†	cor re spond' ence
sand' wich	läugh' a ble‡	cur vi lin' e ar
scull' ion	and' i ron	drȯm' e da ry
ski' vers	an' ec dote	e lec triç' i ty
sky' ey	an' ti dote	ap o deĭc' tic
shrap' nel	an' o dyne	an thro poph' a gī
sol' stice	a pos' *t*le	ar bo res' cent
sol sti' tial	ăr' a besque	ad ven ti' tious
ben' e fice	är' ti san	os ten ta' tious
ben e fi' cial	ax' le-tree	ar gil la' ceous
	bāil' i wick	bi tu' mi nous

* The *u* in *buoyancy* is a consonant, and has the sound of *w*.

† For the *e* silent, in such words as this, see note, page 45.

‡ For the sound of *gh* like *f*, see Exercise 145, page 50.

EXERCISE 483.

soi rée'
(*swä rā'*)
sphinx
pann' ier
tûr' keys
af freight'
bas' tile
bay' ou
bi jou'
(*be zhoo'*)
ca' lyx
chal' ice
col lapse'
dig' it
crup' per
cut' lass

belles-let' tres
(*bel let' ter*)
bo' re as
can' til late
cap-a-pie'
căr' a way
cär nĕl' ian
cor' al lite
coun' ter feit
croc' o dile
cyl' in der
de vel' op
dȳ nam' ies
ep' i taph
eq' ui page
em ploy e'

aux il' ia ry
är' mil la ry
cal is then' ics
chi căn' er y
cŏr' ol la ry
di a pa' son
el e cam pane'
e phem' e ra
es' pi on age
eū lo' gi um
ev a nes' cent
fos' sil iz ed
ho me op' a thy }
ho mœ op' a thy }
ho me o path' ic }
ho mœ o path' ic }

EXERCISE 484.

weird
dis train'
de duce'
ob tuse'
es chew'
fau' cet
flip' pant
gal loon'
hăr' ass
laun' dry
lack' ey
cop' sy
neigh' ing
os' trich
on' slaught

făr' ri er
cou' ri er
flag' eo let
frank in' cense
Hot' ten tot
hȳ e' na
hī a' tus
hȳ drau' lics
im pan' el
in' va lid*
in val' id
hŏl' i day*
hō' ly day
rē cre ate'*
rĕc' re ate

def a ma' tion
in flam ma' tion†
an' a gram
pro' gramme†
I sos' ce les
lin' sey-wool sey
Med i ter ra' ne an
met a mor' pho sis
no men clăt' ure
os cil la' tion
par al lel' o gram
pa ral' y sis
pe cūn' ia ry
per ti na' cious
fo li a' ceous

* Notice, in these words, *in'valid*, *inval'id*, etc., the differences in *meaning*, indicated by differences in *pronunciation*.

† Notice that *inflammation* and *programme*, unlike *inflame* and *anagram*, retain both the *m's* of the original words whence they are derived. Compare note on page 153.

EXERCISE 485.

pāil′ fuls
par′ rot
pen′ non
plant′ ain
pŏm′ mel
pot′ sherd
shep′ *h*erd
prom′ ise
qua drille′
rogu′ ish
sa′ tyr
spher′ ule*
stan′ çhion
strych′ nine
vi*g*n ette′ (*yet*)
venge′ ance

in′ ter stice
jol′ li ty
jūi′ ci ness
ker′ o sene
lab′ y rinth
leth′ ar gy
lo gi′ cian
mal fēa′ sance
māin′ te nance
măr′ i time
mas *q*uer ade′
al le′ giance
I tal′ ic
Mich′ ael mas
mil′ li ner
ver ba′ tim

phar ma çeū′ tic
py ro tech′ nics
re sus′ ci tate
reç i ta tïve′
sphe riç′ i ty
stu pe fac′ tion
ste′ re o scope
ter res′ tri al
vi vaç′ i ty
zo o log′ ic al
a be ce da′ ri an
ac a de mi′ cian
am mu ni′ tion
an nex a′ tion
an tiç i pa′ tīon
bel la don′ na

EXERCISE 486.

trunn′ ion
to′ paz
syr′ inge
sur tout′
sou çhong′
sleigh′ ing
sär′ dïne
sap′ phire
(*saf′ īre*)
saf′ fron
sack′ but
ra gout′
purs′ lain
pul′ leys
re cede′†
ex ceed′†

vend′ i ble
sāl′ a ble
tyr′ an nous
um bra′ geous
tre pan′ ning
te na′ cious
tes ta′ ceous
syn′ the sis
Syr′ i an
syn′ a gogue
sus pi′ cion
tac ti′ cian
sûr cin′ gle
sur veil′ lance
an te cede′
su per sede′

cach in na′ tion
cas′ u ist ry
ca tas′ tro phe
cen trif′ u gal
cen trip′ e tal
ce ru′ le an
cen ten′ ni al
ve ne′ re al
ar te′ ri al
val e dic′ to ry
tau tol′ o gy
su per cil′ i ous
sac ri le′ gious
ir re lig′ ious
con trōl′ la ble
con sōl a ble′

* What is the meaning of the suffix *ule?* See Exercise 454, page 143.

† In *exceed*, *proceed*, and *succeed*, the radical part is written *ceed*, while in *recede* and other words from the same root, it is always written *cede*.

EXERCISE 437.

prov′ ost
pres′ tige
pou drette′
pla cärd′
par têrre′
of fense′
o′ nyx
nes′ cience
na′ iad
in′ nate
jug′ gler
hal loo′
gun′ wale
gram′ mar
stam′ mer
gauz′ y
gawk′ y

i′ ci cle
suav′ i ty
sub′ tle ty
(*sut′ l ty*)
ste′ ve dore
stud′ y ing
sin′ ew y
She ki′ nah
ces sa′ tion
se ces′ sion
Sad′ du cee
rogu′ er y
r*h*yth′ mic al
res tau rant′
(*res to räng′*)
ac qui esce′
ap′ o gee

sep′ a ra ble
pro pi′ ti ate
prop a gan′ dist
pred e ces′ sor
pol y pet′ al ous
phre nol′ o gy
phil o pe′ nä
ôr′ tho e py
o le ag′ i nous
om niv′ o rous
night′ in gale
Nic a ra′ guä
mu niç′ i pal
met a phys′ ies
me diç′ i nal
mĕas′ ūr a bly
le vi′ a than

EXERCISE 438.

g*h*ōst′ ly
ga zelle′
en core′
(*ong kōr′*)
dis sēize′
drach′ mä
cro çhet′ (*shā*)
crotch′ et
cov′ ey
cool′ ly
coo′ ly }
coo′ lie }
bom′ byx
bis′ muth
bil′ ious
bat′ tling
fat′ ling

ag′ gran dize
ad ver tise′
an′ gli cize
ap′ o the*g*m
ap′ pe tite
aq′ ui line
är′ go sy
är′ mis tice
as bes′ tine
at tri′ tion
bil′ let doux
(*bill′ le doo*)
cap u çhin′
co la′ tion
col la′ tion
co quet′ tish*
sug gest′ ive

liq ue fac′ tion
lab′ o ra to ry
ī so thĕrm′ al
jux ta po si′ tion
in ter mit′ tent
in de struc′ ti ble
in āl′ ien a ble
Mis sis sip′ pi
nec′ ro man cy
ob scen′ i ty
pan a ce′ ȧ
pen ny roy′ al
per i hēl′ ion
phan tas ma go′ ri a
phle bot′ o my
phys i ol′ o gy
prep a ra′ tion

* Why is the *t* doubled in *coquettish*, and not in *suggestive?* See Rule VII, page 61; also Rule VIII, page 63.

EXERCISE 489.

trel′ lis	hĕr′ o ine	mal′ le a ble
trĕil′ lage	hel′ le bore	*p*sȳ ɕhol′ o gy
wee′ v*i*l	cū′ pho ny	e rās′ i ble
ast*h*′ mȧ	ha rangu′ ing	cat′ er pil lar
guä′ no	be′ he moth	cas′ so wa ry
(*guä′ no*)	ar rāi*g*n′ ment	ac côr′ di on
whin′ ock	ar te′ ṣian	Æ o′ li an
ve dette′	at′ ti tude	me lo′ de on
ve neer′	be at′ i tude	prom′ is so ry
sôr′ tiē	con du′ cive	rā ti oç i na′ tion
ha̤w′ thorn	con clu′ sive	sc*h*iṣ mat′ ic al
qui′ nine	cor du roy′	sī de′ re al
py′ thon	cre′ o sote	sēn iŏr′ i ty
pȳr′ r*h*ic	*m*ne mon′ ics*	sub ter ra′ ne ous
punch′ eon	coun′ sel or	ac ri mo′ ni ous
āp′ ish	coun′ cil or	ɕo lil′ o quize

EXERCISE 490.

ōw′ ing	ēaveṣ′ drop per	yeō′ man ry
britz′ skȧ	ef fer vesce′	syn ec′ do ɕhe
(*bris′ ka*)	el lip′ sis	a cat a lec′ tic
bo hēa′	em bra′ ṣure	ac cla ma′ tion
ca nāille′	ex cheq′ *u*er	ad sci ti′ tious
co ba̤lt′	an nul′ ment	ac u i′ tion
drȧughts′ man	ful fill′ ment	Ar e op′ a gus
hough′ *e*d (*hŏkt*)	as phal′ tum	ho mol′ o gous
ex scind′	at ta ç̣he′ (*-shā*)	ar ma dil′ lo
fa′ cial	a̤u′ gu ry	as si du′ i ty
fas çïne′	a̤u′ spi ceṣ	as sim′ i late
paġ′ eant	ax′ i om	a dä′ gi o
pi′ broɕh	max′ i mum	al′ le go ry
pre′ ci̤ncts	bag a telle′	an aɕh′ ro niṣm
pro′ logue	Bed′ o̤u ïnṣ	an no ta′ tion
spe′ ciēṣ	bērg′ a mot	an te di lu′ vi an
spīke′ nard	bob bin et′	an tith′ e sis

* Names of sciences ending in *ics* (see Exercise 451, page 142), are, in *form* and in *fact*, *plurals*, though, in present *usage*, mostly treated as *singular*. Some of them, however, as *logic*, *arithmetic*, still retain the singular *form*.

EXERCISE 491.

te′ trarch	cen′ o taph	cha lyb′ e ate
tȳ phoon′	Gen o ēse′*	char i ot eer′
vac′ cine	chi me′ rȧ	cor′ al li form
wrink′ led	chic′ co ry	Cin cin na′ ti
y clep′ ed	daf′ fo dil	chi rog′ ra phy
ep′ i logue	del′ e ble	col lo′ qui al
es′ say ist	in del′ i ble	Con nect′ i cut
ed′ dy ing	de ri′ sive	cy lin′ dric al
em′ bry o	co ēr′ cive	de lir′ i ous
ex′ tir pate	dēr′ ni er	deg ra da′ tion
fär′ ci cal	des′ ic cate	des e cra′ tion
fī bril′ lous	ves ′i cate	dis si pa′ tion
fil′ i gree	di′ o cese	dis ci plin a′ ri an
fla min′ go	quin tes′ sence	di shev′ el ed
fï nä′ le	pu tres′ cence	e clâir′ cisse ment
fruit′ er er	pu is′ sance	mȳr′ tle-ber ry

EXERCISE 492.

fu ga′ cious	dog′ ḡer el	ef flo res′ cence
fī la′ ceous	em′ a nate	en cy clo pe′ di ȧ
fûr′ be low	e lim′ i nate	e piph′ a ny
Ga la′ tians	es cutch′ eon	per cēiv′ a ble
gal′ ax y	Al ge rïne′	re priēv′ a ble
ḡib′ ber ish	fen′ ci ble	me te or ol′ o gy
gri mal′ kin	de fen′ si ble	pu tres′ ci ble
härd′ i hood	frȯnt′ is piece	sab ba ta′ ri an
hav′ er sack	hip′ po drome	scur ril′ i ty
hăr′ ass ing	jour′ ney ing	Sept′ u a gint
Hel′ les pont	Ma dēi′ rȧ	sep ten′ ni al
hem′ is tich	ma li′ cious	te nāil′ lon (-yun)
hem′ stitch	marl a′ ceous	tic-dou lou reux′
her′ e sy	mär′ chion ess	u til i ta′ ri an
in i′ tial	min′ strel sy	un păr′ al lel ed
of fi′ cial	mis′ tle toe	un der pin′ ning

* The ending *ese* (*pertaining to*, or *native of*) is added to names of *places* to form derivative nouns and adjectives; as, Siamese, *pertaining to*, or *native of* Siam. If the final letter in the name is a *vowel*, in the derivative, it is dropped; as, (Vienna+ese) Viennese.

EXERCISE 493.

lēi′ sūre ly	myr′ mi don	ac ro bat′ ic
lar *gh*et′ to	ne′ o phyte	ach ro mat′ ic
li tig′ ious	non çha lance′	ac cel′ er ate
mad′ re pore	māin′ te nance*	ac qui es′ cing
mär′ tyr dom	oc′ u list	Am phic′ ty ons
mill ion âire′	ôr′ ches trȧ	an ni hi la′ tion
myr′ i ad	Od′ ys sey	as sas si na′ tion
mir′ ror *e*d	oph′ thal my	cab ri o let′
nau′ se ate (*-she-*)	pa la′ tial	cen′ te na ry
nau′ ti lus	par′ ox ysm	cer ti o ra′ rī
op ti′ cian	skep′ ti cism	chal ced′ o ny
Or′ phe us	mi*g*n on nette′	chro nol′ o gy
phos′ phor ous	(*min yon et′*)	mat i nee′ (*-nā*)
pa py′ rus	mys′ ti cism	dis ser ta′ tion
ox′ y gen	om nis′ cient	dis cērn′ i ble
or′ to lan	oph′ i cleīde	dis cre′ tion a ry

EXERCISE 494.

păr′ al lax	pär′ lia ment	ef frônt′ e ry
pär′ ley ing	pep′ per idge	eū roc′ ly don
lev′ y ing	Phryġ′ i an	ex haust′ i ble
pic a yune′	pic tur esque′	ex sic ca′ tion
pil′ la ging	pro′ te ge (*-zhā*)	fac-sim′ i le
pit′ ted	mo men′ tous	fas ci na′ tion
pit′ i *e*d	pro spec′ tus	gal′ li nip per
pit′ y ing	pir ou ette′	hal lu ci na′ tion
pil′ lo ry	pȳr′ a mid	ha bēr′ ge on
pôr′ phy ry	quar′ an tïne	her me neū′ tics
preç′ i pice	quĕr′ u lous	guär an tee′ ing
pro ceed′ ing	quī e′ tus	hȳ pēr′ bo le
re cēd′ ing	ras*p*′ ber ry	ich thy ol′ o gy
pro bos′ cis	mer′ chan dise	Im man′ u el
pros′ e lyte	re mit′ tance	hȳ men e′ al
pōrte′ môn nāie	re mit′ tent	ir re sist′ i ble

* Note that, in forming *maintenance* from *maintain*, *ai*, in the latter, has been changed to *e*; and that often a *medial* vowel or *diphthong* is either thus exchanged for some other vowel, or altogether omitted; as, in *proclamation* from *proclaim*, *arbitrate*, (not *arbiterate*), from *arbiter*.

EXERCISE 495.

pōrt man′ teau (*to*)	ap pel′ lant	met a phy si′ cian
pàsse-par tout′	re pel′ lent	dec a he′ dron*
Gal′ i lee	sac′ ri lege	as a fet′ i dà }
preç′ e dence	os′ tra cize	as a fœt′ i dà }
rec′ om pense	su per vise′	ne fa′ ri ous
re gat′ tà	sym′ pho ny	cu ta′ ne ous
reş er voir′ (*vwôr*)	re vẽr′ sion	dī ar *rhe*′ à }
ru bes′ cent	pa tri′ cian	dī ar *rhœ*′ à }
şub pœ′ nà	vo li′ tion	Pro me′ the an
sär′ do nyx	tẽr′ mi nus	Si cil′ i an
sat′ ir ist	lu′ mi nous	pro thon′ o ta ry
sŏm′ er sault }	tete-à-tete′	speç i fi ca′ tion
sŏm′ er set }	tit′ il late	Terp si*ch*′ o re
sep′ a rate	tŏngue′-tīed	spon ta ne′ i ty
op′ er ate	va nil′ là	saġ it ta′ ri us

EXERCISE 496.

sham poo′ ing	vẽr′ ga lieu }	al lop′ a thy
strat′ e gy	vẽr′ ga loo }	an tiç i pa′ tion
stra te′ gic	vīr′ gou leūse	a poth′ e ca ry
sto′ i cişm	wag′ on er	as sim i la′ tion
spe′ cial ty	por′ rin ger	dis sim u la′ tion
stŏm′ a cher	whīrl′ i gig	Ath e ne′ um }
aē′ ġis	bla′ zon ry	Ath e næ′ um }
ēa′ glet	al′ ka line	can thăr′ i deş
be dim′ med	am bro′ şial	col lo ca′ tion
be grīm′ ed	aph′ o rişm	cor nu co′ pi à
can non ade′	au′ spi ceş	cor rel′ a tive
*ch*or′ is ter	bac′ *ch*a nal	dī ag no′ sis
cin′ na mon	Beth′ pha ge	del e te′ ri ous
cic′ a trīze	co′ cōa-nut	der e lic′ tion
dis fran′ chīşe	col′ o cynth	ig nīt′ i ble
cock′ a trīce	sac′ *ch*a rine	in dīct′ a ble
com′ mo dore	Co los′ sus	as sid′ u ous

* Words ending in *hedron*, *hedral*, *hĕdrous* (from *hĕdra*, a Greek word signifying a *seat*, *side*, or *base*), are sometimes, though improperly, written without the *h*; a *polyedron*, *tetraëdon*, etc. See Exercise 286.

EXERCISE 497.

ɇhris′ *ten* dom	le′ o nīne	hȳ poth′ e cate
clâir voy′ ant	Lyd′ i an	a chiēv′ a ble
co los′ sal*	coun ter poiṣe′	comp trōl′ ler (-*con*)
Co los′ sianṣ	cyn′ o ṣụre	em bel′ lish ment
cu ras′ sōw	def′ i cit	in gra′ ti ate
*C*za rï′ nȧ	dis em bogue′	ne go′ ti ate
tat′ ting	mol′ li ent	dī a pho ret′ ic
Mat′ thew	cuï ras siēr′	hȳ dran′ ge ȧ
strip′ ling	cat′ er waul	in i′ ti ate
rip′ pling	bron̲′ ɇhi al	e nun ci′ ate
whit′ tling	Bo′ na parte	in diġ′ e nous
wit′ ling	cau′ ter ize	ven tril′ o quy
quăg′ gȧ	rec′ og nize	de mar ka′ tion } †
quăg′ ḡy	mar′ ble ize*	de mar ca′ tion }
taç′ it ly	Neph′ tha lim	pro vōk′ a ble†
des′ ue tude	thrĕat′ *en* ing	prov o ca′ tion†
den′ ti frïce	whêr ev′ er	rev′ o ca ble

EXERCISE 498.

di lem′ mȧ	whêre with al′	an tip′ o dēṣ
dom′ i nie	trụ′ cu lent	fo li a′ ceous
E ne′ id	dow′ a ġer	Mag da le′ ne
eçh′ e lon	en tram′ mel	pal′ li a tive
ex′ ple tive	en roll′ ment	măr′ rïage a ble
ex′ qui ṣite	es cri toire′ (-*twor*)	fer ru′ gi nous
fla gi′ tious	Es′ qui maux	in ef′ fa ble
jụ di′ cious	(*Es′ ke mōz*)	in fal′ li ble
găr′ ri son	fa ri′ nȧ	in oc′ u late
gloss′ a ry	fi nan ciēr′	ir i des′ cent
fôr′ feit ure	san̲ ga ree′	ir rep′ a ra ble
moun tain eer′	hy′ a cinth	in a ni′ tion
hal berd iēr′	im′ mi nent	in sid′ i ous
mu le teer′	em′ i nent	o vip′ a rous
hâre′ lip ped	jag u ar′	lu gu′ bri ous
hâir′-dress er	ju′ gu lar	leg′ is la tive

* *Marbleize* is formed from *marble* and *ize*, but without dropping the *e* in *marble*, according to Rule X, page 67.

† Notice the interchange of *c* and *k* in these words.

EXERCISE 499.

guil' le mot
Hab' ak kuk
här' le quin (*-kin*)
ha' zel-nut
im' mi grant
em' i grant
me men' tōs
su per car' goes*
Ot' to mans
syn' co pe
pa lä' ver
pel lu' cid
phleg mat' ic
pick' er el
ple' o nasm
pôr' ce lain

con nec' tion†
com plex' ion
lith' o graph
moï' e ty
ex po se' (*-zā*)
naught' i ness
non pa rĕil'
or' re ry
o ver-rate'
păr' a phrase
pha' e ton
pho' to graph
pin' a fore
pome gran' ate
pōr' trait ūre
choc' o late

mo not' o nous
ol fac' to ry
oc ten' ni al
pen in' su lȧ
zig' zag ḡer y
a cot y le' don
an æs thet' ic
ap o the' o sis
an thel min' tic
ar chæ ol' o gy
ap' o plex y
dys' en ter y
pres' by ter y
hī e ro glyph' ies
hȳ dro path' ic
al lo path' ic

EXERCISE 500.

pōs til' ion
mo dill' ion
pre cēd' ing
ex ceed' ing
pro cēd' ure
ad hēr' ing
en dēar' ing
ag' gre gate
am' phi brach
an cho' vy
anch' or age
as cen' sion
de ten' tion
ban dit' tī
be siēġ' ing
chin chil' lȧ
chro mat' ic

prom e nade'
Pyth' i an
re veil' le (*-yā*)
re splen' dence
at tend' ance
round' de lay
sele rot' ic
se di' tious
sus pi' cious
syz' y gy
suc' cu lence
an' nu lar
aph' yl lous
A pol' lo
ap' o logue
re cēipt' ed
un yiēld' ing

phos phor es'cence
cor po' re al
cor rōd' i ble
ep' i lep sy
e qui noc' tial
ex' pi a to ry
gul li bil' i ty
in fin i tes' i mal
mer e tri' cious
per cep' ti ble
pat ro nym' ic
tit il la' tion
vil' i fy ing
A pol' ly on
a cērb' i ty
an a con' dȧ
a poc' ry phal

* For the plural of words ending in *o*, see Exercise 241, page 73, and the note there.

† On the spelling of this word, see Exercise 278, page 85.

EXERCISE 501.

stel′ lu lar
çhan de liēr′
côr′ ne ȧ
co q*u*et′ ry
cor′ pus çle
s*c*hol′ ar ly
dis pērs′ ing
dis bûrs′ ing
co ēr′ çing
ef′ fi gy
pan′ cre as
mo̤uff′ lon
e quer′ ry }
eq′ ue ry }
en fi lade′
e rāş′ ure

the′ o rize
im pro viş̤e′
crin′ o line
ex ciş′ ion*
re scis′ şion*
sciş′ şorş*
cru̱′ ci ble
cÿn′ ic al
Phi lip′ pī
in *w*rap′ p*e*d
r*h*iz′ o pod
e′ qui poişe
es pouş′ al
bel-es prït′ (-*pree*)
bȯm ba zïne′ }
bȯm ba şine′ }

as cer tāin′ ing
bri tan′ ni ȧ
cat′ a lep sy
cir cu′ i tous
chas tīş′ a ble
con de scen′ sion
cor rob o ra′ tion
cor y phe′ us
cru ci fix′ ion
pĕr′ emp to ry
e liç′ it ing
en gi neer′ ing
fin an ciēr′ ing
ex′ cel len cy
ex hu ma′ tion
ca paç′ i tate

EXERCISE 502.

es chew̆′ *e*d
re view̆′ *e*d
sub du′ *e*d
mĭr′ a cle
mȳ̆r′ i arch
fore run′ ner
gĭ raffe′
Ca′ ia phas
smell′-less†
gut′ tur al
he gi′ rȧ
pur vẹy′ or
ho′ şier y
hun̠′ gri ly
hy′ dro gen
hom′ o nym

U lys sēş
gon do liēr′
grȧss′ hop per
harp′ si chord
hec′ a to̤m*b*
hep′ tarch y
hy ge′ ian
ir′ ri gate
i*s*l′ and er
jac′ o net
Gēr′ g̱e neş
in ēr′ ti ȧ
lieū ten′ ant
maç′ er ate
ma ra̤u′ der
ne phrït′ ic

E paph ro di′ tus
en dēav′ or ing
dis sev′ er ing
in′ no cen cy
leġ er de māin′
me̤ tron′ o my
jan′ i za ry
oph thal′ mi ȧ
per ad vent′ ure
phra şe ol′ o gy
pick′ a nin ny
sēi*g*n eū′ ri al
fi du′ ci a ry
su per an′ nu a ted
ve ne sec′ tion
per i pa tet′ ic

* The radical parts *cision* in *decision*, and *scission* in *rescission* are from different roots, or different forms of the same root. From the latter we get, also, *scissors* (*cutters*), *scissure*, *abscission*, and some others.

† For words of this class, see Rule IX, with the note on page 66.

EXERCISE 503.

mil′ le ped } *	oc′ ci put	pa rish′ ion er
mil′ le pede }	o′ ce lot	pe ti′ tion er
es sen′ tials	o ver-run′	mil le na′ ri an
im pūgn′ ing	me phit′ ic	than a top′ sis
per′ qui site	trav′ ers ing	syc′ o phan cy
Ca′ naan ite	ut′ ter most	sī mul ta′ ne ous
sew′ er age	se cêd′ er	sym met′ ric al
de mul′ cent	shad′ ow ing	syn co pa′ tion
sha moy′ ing	ser ra′ tion	text′ u a ry
shôr′ ling	sem′ a phore	Ar is ti′ dēs
Shi′ lōh	Ten′ e riffe	seq ues tra′ tion
shin′ ney	yt′ tri um	sĕr′ i cult ure
spin′ ach }	wāin′ scot ing	ther mom′ e ter
spin′ age }	synch′ ro nism	the od′ o lite
Ses os′ tris	toûr′ na ment	the o lo′ gi an
A chil′ lēs	sûr′ feĭt ed	u biq′ ui tous

EXERCISE 504.

sed′ litz	so bri quet′ (-*kā*)	ac′ cli ma ted
syn′ o nym	Al mīght′ y	a mal′ gam ate
viç′ i nage	An′ ti christ	af fa bil′ i ty
mos *quï*′ to	är′ go naut	at trib′ u ta ble
um bra′ geous	at′ mos phere	bī og′ ra phy
unct′ u ous	philo gis′ ton	bī en′ ni al
syn op′ sis	et′ a gere (-*zhâr*)	qua tĕr′ ni on
sta tis′ ties	like′ li hood	con san guin′ i ty
skel′ e ton	Bab′ y lon	cor ru ga′ tion
scăr′ i fy	bal′ us ter	con tro vĕr′ sial
ter′ ri er	ca taw′ bȧ	dē fal ca′ tion
sti let′ to	cal a boose′	de clam′ a to ry
ad′ ju tant	Xen′ o phon	in flam′ ma to ry
a phēl′ ion	ex am′ ine	civ′ il iz ed
ăr′ ro gant	fil′ li beg	e lec triç′ i ty
är′ chi trave	tram′ mel ing	mulct′ u a ry
at′ ro phy	fic ti′ tious	mul ti pliç′ i ty

* Words ending in *ped* (Latin *pes*, *pedis*, *a foot*), are sometimes written with a final *e*, as *millepede*. The best authorities, however, write them all without the *e*, like *biped* and *quadruped*. See Exercise 286, page 87.

EXERCISE 505.

brig′ an tine
cin na bar
cop′ y ist
dis cre′ tion
dī gres′ sion
diș çẽrn′ ment
dul′ ci mer
ex′ pi ate
el′ e phant
fal set′ to
fēaș′ i ble
as′ tra gal
bal′ us trade
con sum′ mate
glyç′ er ine
id′ i o cy

fan dan′ go
hem′ or *rh*oidș
hôrse′ whip ping
ho șan′ nȧ
jan′ i tor
leg′ i ble
mag′ net ism
me theg′ lin
musk′ mel on
im brue′ ment
un tru′ ly
re çher çhe′
(*rŭh sher shā′*)
col′ chi chum
pär′ quet ry
Sis′ y phus

in ex′ o ra ble
in i ti a′ tion
in stan ta′ ne ous
i tin′ er a cy
dul cam′ a rȧ
ex e get′ ic al
ex tra′ ne ous
gen e al′ o gy
heb dom′ a dal
si le′ si ȧ
Mel chiș′ e dec
Ar chi me′ dēș
con vey′ ing
in veigh′ ing
hy drom′ e ter
hi bẽr′ ni an

EXERCISE 506.

pil la′ ger
prej′ u dice
se rag*l*′ io
reg′ i men
ret′ ro cede
pem′ mi can
lôr*g*n ette′ (*-yet*)
llä′ mȧ
Mes si′ ah
eū pep′ sy
feūd′ al ișm
fort′ nīght
pȳr′ *rh*o nișm
chlo′ rīde*
i′ o dīne*
cro quet′ (*-kā*)

fu șil lade′
mis′ chiev ous
nä′ ïve te (*-tā*)
Nin′ e veh
nu′ cle us
o′ gre ish
out ra′ geous
off′ set ting
pam phlet eer′
pan the′ on
pȧss′ o ver
per sim′ mon
pec′ ca ry
pend′ u lum
pŏst′ hu mous
s*ch*iș mat′ ic

laz a ret′ to
lo co mo′ tion
māy′ or al ty
e qui lib′ ri um
eq′ ui ta ble
phil o me′ lȧ
tra pe′ zi um
tra ge′ di an
dem a gŏg′ ic
tran scend ent′ al
Mit y le′ ne
po tas′ si um
reș ur rec′ tion
ca mel′ o pard
tri um′ vi rate
som nam′ bu lișm

* *Chloride* and *iodine* are representatives of a class of chemical terms, in respect to which usage has been variable; most of them having been formerly written without the *e* final. The *e* is now generally retained in them all, except the word *tannin*. See Exercise 286, page 87.

SECTION XXIV.

NAMES OF PERSONS, WITH THEIR SIGNIFICATION.

MALES.

EXERCISE 507.

A'ARON (*âr'un*), lofty; inspired.
A'BEL, breath; vanity.
A BI'JAH, to whom Jehovah is a father.
AB'NER, father of light.
A'BRA HAM, father of a multitude.
AB'SA LOM, father of peace.
AD'AM, earth-man; red earth.
A'DIN, tender; delicate; soft.
AD O NI'RAM, Lord of hight.
AL'BERT, nobly bright; illustrious.
AL EX AN'DER, a defender of men.
AL'FRED, good counselor.
AL'MON, hidden.
A LON'ZO, AL PHON'SO, all ready; willing.
AL'PHE US, exchange.
AL'VIN, beloved of the Lord.
AM'A SA, a burden.
AM'BROSE, immortal; divine.
A'MOS, strong; courageous.
AN'DREW, strong; manly.
AN'THO NY, AN'TO NY, priceless; praiseworthy.
AR'CHI BALD, extremely bold.
AR'NOLD, strong as an eagle.
AR'THUR, high; noble.
A'SA, healer; physician.
ASH'ER, happy; fortunate.
AU GUS'TUS, exalted; imperial.
AZ A RI'AH, helped of the Lord.
BAR'NA BAS, son of corruption.
BAR THOL'O MEW, a warlike son.
BEN'E DICT, blessed.
BEN'JA MIN, son of the right hand.
CA'LEB, a dog.
CAL'VIN, bald.
CE'PHAS, a stone.
CHARLES, strong; manly.
CHRIS'TO PHER, bearing Christ.
CLEM'ENT, mild-temp'd; merciful.

EXERCISE 508.

CON'RAD, bold in counsel; resolute.
CON'STAN TINE, resolute; firm.
COR NE'LI US (*uncertain*).
CY'RUS, the sun.
DAN'IEL, a divine judge.
DA RI'US, preserver.
DA'VID, beloved.
DON'ALD, proud chief.
DUN'CAN, brown chief.
EB EN E'ZER, the stone of help.
ED'GAR, protector of property.
ED'MUND, defender of property.
ED'WARD, guardian of property.
ED'WIN, gainer of property.
EG'BERT, the sword's brightness.
E LE A'ZER, to whom God is a help.
E'LI, a foster son.
E LI'HU, God the Lord.
E LI'JAH, Jehovah is my God.
E LI'SHA, God my salvation.
EL'NA THAN, God gave.
E'NOCH, consecrated; dedicated.
E PHRA IM, very fruitful.
E RAS'TUS, lovely; amiable.
E'THAN, firmness; strength.
EU'GENE, *or* EU GENE', noble.
E ZE'KI EL, strength of God.
EZ'RA, help.
FER'DI NAND, brave; valiant.
FRAN'CIS, *or* FRANK, free.
FRED'ER IC, a peaceful ruler.
GEORGE, a landholder; husbandman.
GID'E ON, a destroyer.
GIL'BERT, yellow-bright; famous.
GILES, a kid.
GOD'FREY, at peace with God.
GOD'WIN, good in war.
GREG'O RY, watchful.
GRIF'FITH, having great faith.
GUS TA'VUS, a warrior; hero.
HE'MAN, faithful.
HEN'RY, the head of a house.

EXERCISE 509.

HER'BERT, glory of the army.
HEZ E KI'AH, strength of the Lord.
HI'RAM, most noble.
HO'MER, a pledge; security.
HOR'ACE, HO RA'TIO, } (*uncertain.*)
HU'BERT, bright in spirit.
HUGH, mind; spirit; soul.
ICH'A BOD, the glory is departed.
I'RA, watchful.
I'SAAC, laughter.
I SA'IAH, salvation of the Lord.
IS'RA EL, a soldier of God.
JA'COB, a supplanter.
JAMES, the same as Jacob.
JA'SON, a healer.
JAS'PER (*uncertain*).
JED E DI'AH, beloved of the Lord.
JER E MI'AH, exalted of the Lord.
JES'SE, wealth,
JO'AB, Jehovah is his father.
JOB, afflicted; presented.
JO'EL, the Lord is God.
JOHN, the gracious gift of God.
JON'A THAN, gift of Jehovah.
JO'SEPH, he shall add.
JOSH'U A, God of salvation.
JO SI'AH, given of the Lord.
JO'THAM, the Lord is upright.
JU'LI US, soft-haired.
LAW'RENCE, crowned with laurel.
LE AN'DER, lion-man.
LEM'U EL, created by God.
LEON'ARD, strong *or* brave as a lion.
LEW'IS, bold warrior.
LU'THER, illustrious warrior.
MAL'A CHI, messenger of the Lord.
MA NAS'SEH, forgetfulness.
MARK, sprung from Mars.
MAR'TIN, of Mars; warlike.
MAT'THEW (*math'thu*), gift of Jehovah
MILES, a soldier.
MI'CHA EL, who is like God?
MOR'GAN, a seaman.
MO'SES, drawn out of the water.
NA'THAN, a gift.

EXERCISE 510.

NA THAN'A EL, the gift of God.
NE HE MI'AH, comfort of the Lord.
NICH'O LAS, victory of the people.
NO'AH, rest; comfort.
NOR'MAN, a native of Normandy.
O'BED, serving God.
OL'I VER, an olive-tree.
OS'CAR, bounding warrior.
PAT'RICK, noble; a patrician.
PAUL, little.
PE'TER, a rock.
PHI LAN'DER, a lover of men.
PHI LE'MON, loving; friendly.
PHIL'IP, a lover of horses.
PHIN'E AS, mouth of brass.
RAPH'A EL, the healing of God.
REU'BEN, behold, a son!
RICH'ARD, rich-hearted; powerful.
ROB'ERT, bright in fame.
ROD'ER IC, rich in fame.
RO DOL'PHUS, famous wolf; hero.
ROG'ER, famous with the spear.
ROW'LAND, fame of the land.
RU'FUS, red; red-haired.
SAM'U EL, heard of God.
SE'BA, eminent.
SETH, appointed.
SIL VA'NUS, living in a wood.
SIL VES'TER, bred in the country.
SIM'E ON, hearing with acceptance.
SOL'O MON, peaceable.
STE'PHEN (*ste'vn*), a crown.
THAD'DE US, the wise.
THE'O DORE, the gift of God.
THE OPH'I LUS, a lover of God.
THOM'AS (*tom'as*), a twin.
TIM'O THY, fearing God.
U LYS'SES, a hater.
U RI'AH, light of the Lord.
VAL'EN TINE, strong; healthy.
VIC'TOR, a conqueror.
VIN'CENT, conquering.
WAL'TER, ruling the host.
WILL'IAM, resolute.
ZACH A RI'AH, remembered of the Lord.
ZE LO'TES, a zealot.
ZE'NAS, gift of Jupiter.
ZEPH A NI'AH, hid of the Lord.

FEMALES.

EXERCISE 511.

AB'I GAIL (*-gel*), my father's joy.
AD'A LINE, } of noble birth; a
AD'E LAIDE, } princess.
AG'NES, chaste; pure.
AL'ICE, a princess.
AL MI'RA, lofty; a princess.
A MAN'DA, worthy to be loved.
A ME'LI A, busy; energetic.
A'MY, beloved.
AN GE LI'NA, lovely; angelic.
ANN, AN'NA, grace.
AN TOI NETTE', inestimable.
AR A BEL'LA, a fair altar.
AU GUS'TA, feminine of Augustus.
AU RO'RA, morning redness.
BER'THA, bright; beautiful.
BLANCH, *or* BLANCHE, white.
CAR'O LINE, feminine of Charles.
CATH'A RINE, pure.
CHAR'LOTTE, feminine of Charles.
CLAR'A, bright; illustrious.
CO'RA, maiden.
COR DE'LI A, warm-hearted.
CYN'THI A, belonging to Mount
DEB'O RAH, a bee. [Cynthus.
DI AN'THA, flower of Jove; a pink.
DOR'CAS, a gazelle.
E'DITH, happiness.
EL'E A NOR, light.
ELIZ'A BETH, *or* E LI'ZA, conse-
EL VI'RA, white. [crated to God.
EM'E LINE, energetic; industrious.
EM'I LY, same as Emeline.
ES'THER (*-ter*), a star; good for-
EU'NICE, happy victory. [tune.
E'VA, EVE, life. [news.
E VAN'GE LINE, bringing glad
FE LIC'I A (*-lish*), happiness.
FI DE'LI A, faithful
FLO'RA, flowers. [ing.
FLOR'ENCE, blooming; flourish-
FRAN'CES, feminine of Francis.
GER'TRUDE, spear-maiden.
GRACE, grace; favor.
HAN'NAH, the same as Anna.
HAR'RI ET, feminine of Henry.

EXERCISE 512.

HEL'EN, light.
HEN RI ET'TA, feminine of Henry.
I'DA, godlike.
I RE'NE, peaceful. [beth.
IS A BEL'LA, the same as Eliza-
JANE, f. of John; same as Joanna.
JE MI'MA, a dove.
JE RU'SHA, possessed.
JO AN'NA, feminine of John.
JO'SEPH INE, feminine of Joseph.
JU'DITH, praised.
JU'LI A, feminine of Julius; soft-
LAU'RA, a laurel. [haired.
LO RIN'DA, variation of Laura.
LOU I'SA, feminine of Louis; bold
LU CRE'TI A, light. [warrior.
LU'CY, f. of Lucius; born at break
LYD'I A, a native of Lydia. [of day.
MAR'GA RET, a pearl.
MA RI'A, the same as Mary.
MAR'THA, the ruler of the house.
MA'RY, bitter; star of the sea.
MA TIL'DA, mighty battle-maid.
ME LIS'SA, a bee.
MIR'I AM, the same as Mary.
NAN'CY, familiar form of Ann.
NO'RA, contraction of Leonora;
OL'IVE, an olive. [light.
PHE'BE, pure; radiant.
RA'CHEL, a ewe.
RE BEC'CA, of enchanting beauty
RO'SA, a rose
RUTH, beauty.
SA'RAH, a princess.
SO PHI'A, wisdom.
SO PHRO'NI A, of a sound mind.
STEL'LA, a star.
SU'SAN, a lily.
THE RE'SA, carrying ears of corn.
TRY PHE'NA, delicate; luxurious.
TRY PHO'SA, luxurious; dainty.
UR'SU LA, she-bear.
VIC TO'RI A, victory.
VIR GIN'I A, virgin; pure.
WIL HEL MI'NA, feminine of
WILHELM or WILLIAM, resolute.

ABBREVIATIONS USED IN WRITING.

A. or Ans.—Answer.
A.—Adjective; Acre.
A. A. S.—Fellow of the American Academy.
A. B. or B. A.—Bachelor of Arts.
A. B. S.—American Bible Society.
Acct.—Account.
A. D.—In the year of our Lord.
Adj.—Adjutant.
Adv.—Adverb.
Agt.—Agent.
Al. or Ala.—Alabama.
Ald.—Alderman.
Alex.—Alexander.
A. M. { Master of Arts; Before Noon; In the year of the world.
Am. or Amer.—American.
Amt.—Amount.
Anon.—Anonymous.
Ant.—Antiquity.
Apr.—April.
Arith.—Arithmetic.
Ark.—Arkansas.
Art.—Article.
Asst.—Assistant.
Atty.—Attorney.
Aug.—August.
Av.—Avenue.
Bal.—Balance.
Bbl.—Barrel.
B. C. or A. C.—Before Christ.
B. D.—Bachelor of Divinity.
Benj.—Benjamin.
Bot.—Botany.
Br. or Bro.—Brother.
B. V.—Blessed Virgin.
C. or Cent.—A hundred.
Cal.—California; Calendar.
Cant.—Canticles.
Caps.—Capitals.
Capt.—Captain.
Cash.—Cashier.
Ch. or Chap.—Chapter.
Chron.—Chronicles.
Co.—Company; County.
Col.—Colonel; Colossians.
Coll.—College; Collector.
Com. { Commissioner; Commodore; Committee; Commerce.
Conj.—Conjunction.
Conn. or Ct.—Connecticut.
Const.—Constable; Constitution.
Cor.—Corinthians.
C. P. S.—Keeper of the Privy Seal.
Cr.—Credit; Creditor.
C. S.—Keeper of the Seal.
Cts.—Cents.
Cwt.—A hundred weight.
Cyc.—Cyclopedia.
Dan.—Daniel; Danish.
D. C.—District of Columbia.
D. D.—Doctor of Divinity.
Dea.—Deacon.
Dec.—December.
Deg.—Degree or Degrees.
Del.—Delaware; Delegate.
Dem.—Democrat.
Den.—Denmark.
Dept.—Deputy; Department.
Deut.—Deuteronomy.
Dft.—Defendant.
Dict.—Dictionary. Dictator.
Dist.—District.
Do. or Ditto.—The same.
Dols.—Dollars.
Doz.—Dozen.
Dr.—Doctor; Debtor.
E.—East; Earl.
Eccl.—Ecclesiastes.
Ed.—Editor; Edition.
e. g.—For example.
E. I.—East Indies.
Eliz.—Elizabeth.
Encyc.—Encyclopedia.
Eng.—England; English.
Ep.—Epistle.
Eph.—Ephesians.
Esq.—Esquire.
Etc. or &c.—And so forth.
Ex.—Example; Exodus.
Exr.—Executor.
Ezek.—Ezekiel.
Fahr.—Fahrenheit.
Feb.—February.

Fem.—Feminine.
Fig.—Figure.
Fl.—Flemish; Florida.
Fr.—France; French.
F. R. S.—Fellow of the Royal Society.
F. S. A.—Fellow of the Society of Arts.
Ft.—Foot; Feet; Fort.
Fur.—Furlong.
Ga.—Georgia.
Gal.—Galatians.
G. B.—Great Britain.
Gen.—Genesis; General.
Gent.—Gentlemen.
Geo.—George; Georgia
Geog.—Geography.
Geol.—Geology.
Geom.—Geometry.
Ger.—German.
Gov.—Governor.
Gr.—Greek; Grain; Gross.
Hab.—Habakkuk.
Hag.—Haggai.
H. B. M.—His or her Britannic Majesty.
Hdkf.—Handkerchief.
Heb.—Hebrews.
Hhd.—Hogshead.
Hist.—History.
Hon.—Honorable.
H. R.—House of Representatives.
Hund.—Hundred.
Ib. or Ibid.—In the same place.
Id.—The same.
i. e.—That is.
I. H S.—Jesus, the Savior of Men.
Ill.—Illinois.
Incog.—Unknown.
Ind.—Indiana.
Inst.—Instant; or the present month.
Int.—Interest.
Inter.—Interjection.
Io.—Iowa.
Isa.—Isaiah.
It.—Italy; Italian.
Jan.—January.
Jer.—Jeremiah.
Josh.—Joshua.
J. P.—Justice of the Peace.
Jr. or Jun.—Junior.
Kan.—Kansas.
Ky.—Kentucky.
L.—Lord; Lady; Latin.
La.—Louisiana.
Lat.—Latitude.
lbs.—Pounds in weight.
Leg.—Legislature.
Lev.—Leviticus.
Lieut.—Lieutenant.
L. I.—Long Island.
LL.D.—Doctor of Laws.
Lon.—Longitude.
Lou. or La.—Louisiana.
L. S.—Place of the Seal.
M.—Meridian; Thousand.
Ma. or Minn.—Minnesota.
Mad.—Madam.
Maj.—Major.
Masc.—Masculine.
Mass.—Massachusetts.
Math.—Mathematics.
Matt.—Matthew.
M. B.—Bachelor of Physic.
M. C.—Member of Congress.
M. D.—Doctor of Physic.
Md.—Maryland.
Mdlle.—Mademoiselle.
Me.—Maine.
Mem.—Memorandum.
Messrs.—Gentlemen; Sirs.
Mex.—Mexico; Mexican.
Mich.—Michigan; Michael.
Minn.—Minnesota.
Miss.—Mississippi.
Mo.—Missouri.
Mons.—Monsieur.
M. P.—Member of Parliament.
Mr.—Master or Mister.
Mrs.—Mistress (*pron.*) missis.
MS.—Manuscript.
MSS.—Manuscripts.
Mt.—Mount or Mountain.
Myth.—Mythology.
N.—North.
N. A.—North America.
N. B.—Take notice.
N. C.—North Carolina.
N. E.—New England; North-east.
Neb.—Nebraska.
Neh.—Nehemiah.
N. H.—New Hampshire.
N. J.—New Jersey.
No.—Number.
Nom.—Nominative.

Nov.—November.
N. S.—New Style ; Nova Scotia.
N. T.—New Testament.
Num.—Numbers.
N. W.—North-west.
N. Y.—New York.
O.—Ohio.
Obad.—Obadiah.
Obj.—Objective ; Objection.
Obt.—Obedient.
Oct.—October.
O. S.—Old Style.
O. T.—Old Testament.
Oz.—Ounce or ounces.
P., pp.—Page, pages.
Pa. or Penn.—Pennsylvania.
Parl.—Parliament.
Per or pr.—By the ; as, *per* yard.
Per cent.—By the hundred.
Pet.—Peter.
Phil.—Philip ; Philippians.
Phil.—Philadelphia.
Philom.—Lover of learning.
P. M.—Post Master ; Afternoon.
P. O.—Post Office.
Pop.—Population.
Pos.—Possessive.
Prep.—Preposition.
Pres.—President.
Prob.—Problem.
Prof.—Professor.
Pro. tem.—For the time being.
Prov.—Proverbs.
P. S.—Post-script.
Pwt.—Pennyweight.
Q.—Queen ; Question.
Q. E. D.—Which was to be demonstrated.
Q. E. F.—Which was to be done.
Qr.—Quarter.
q. s.—A sufficient quantity.
Qt.—Quart.
Rec'd.—Received.
Regt.—Regiment.
Rep.—Representative.
Rev.—Revelations ; Reverend.
R. I.—Rhode Island.
Rom.—Romans.
R. R.—Railroad.
Rt. Hon.—Right Honorable.
Rt. Rev.—Right Reverend.
S.—South.
S. A.—South America.
Sam.—Samuel.
Sat.—Saturday.
S. C.—South Carolina.
Schr.—Schooner.
Scot.—Scotland.
Sec.—Section ; Secretary.
S. E.—South-east.
Sen.—Senator ; Senior.
Sept.—September.
Serg.—Sergeant.
Servt.—Servant.
Sol.—Solomon ; Solution.
Sp.—Spain ; Spanish.
ss.—To wit ; namely.
St.—Saint ; Street.
S. T. D.—Doctor of Divinity.
Sun.—Sunday.
Supt.—Superintendent.
S. W.—South-west.
Ter.—Territory.
Tenn.—Tennessee.
Tex.—Texas.
Theo.—Theodore.
Theol.—Theology.
Thess.—Thessalonians.
Thurs.—Thursday.
Tim.—Timothy.
Tit.—Titus.
Tr.—Translation ; Treasurer.
Ult.—The last, or last month.
U. S.—United States.
U. S. A. { United States of America ; United States Army.
U. S. N.—United States Navy.
U. T.—Utah Territory.
V. or Vide.—See ; refer to.
V.—Verse ; Verb.
Va.—Virginia.
Viz.—To wit ; namely.
Vol.—Volume.
V. P.—Vice President.
vs.—Against.
Vt.—Vermont.
W.—West.
Wed.—Wednesday.
W. I.—West Indies.
Wis.—Wisconsin.
Wm.—William.
Wt.—Weight.
Yd.—Yard.
Zool.—Zoology.

ROMAN AND ARABIC NOTATION.

Roman.	Arabic.		Roman.	Arabic.	
I	1	one	XXX	30	thirty
II	2	two	XL	40	forty
III	3	three	L	50	fifty
IV	4	four	LX	60	sixty
V	5	five	LXX	70	seventy
VI	6	six	LXXX	80	eighty
VII	7	seven	XC	90	ninety
VIII	8	eight	C	100	1 hundred
IX	9	nine	CC	200	2 hundred
X	10	ten	CCC	300	3 hundred
XI	11	eleven	CCCC	400	4 hundred
XII	12	twelve	D	500	5 hundred
XIII	13	thirteen	DC	600	6 hundred
XIV	14	fourteen	DCC	700	7 hundred
XV	15	fifteen	DCCC	800	8 hundred
XVI	16	sixteen	DCCCC	900	9 hundred
XVII	17	seventeen	M	1000	1 thousand
XVIII	18	eighteen	MDCCCLXVIII		1868; one thousand eight hundred sixty-eight.
XIX	19	nineteen			
XX	20	twenty			
XXI	21	twenty-one			

All the different numbers are expressed by various combinations of the seven letters I. V. X. L. C. D. M. A letter of a less value placed before one of a greater, is to be subtracted from it; placed after, it is to be added to it, thus:—

V	five	X	ten	L	fifty	C	a hundred.
IV	four	IX	nine	XL	forty	XC	ninety
VI	six	XI	eleven	LX	sixty	CX	hundred and ten.

FOREIGN WORDS AND PHRASES.

Ab in i'ti o.—From the beginning.
Ad cap tan'dum.—To attract.
Ad fi'nem.—To the end.
Ad hom'i nem.—To the man.
Ad in fi ni'tum.—Without limit.
Ad lib'i tum.—At pleasure.
Ad rem.—To the point.
Ad va lo'rem.—According to val- [ue.
A li as.—Otherwise.
Al'i bi.—Elsewhere.
Al ma mā'ter.—A cherishing mother. [our Lord.
An'no Dom'i ni.—In the year of
An no mun'di.—In the year of the world.
An'gli ce.—In English.
An'i mus.—Mind; feeling.
Beau i de'al.—A perfect model of beauty.
Beau monde.—The gay world.
Bon ton.—The hight of fashion.
Bo'na fi'de.—In good faith.
Cap-a-piē'.—From head to foot.
Ca put.—Head; chapter. [plenty.
Cor'nu co'pi a.—The horn of
Coup d'état (koo da tä').—A stroke of policy. [is it?
Cui bo'no.—For whose benefit
De fac'to.—In fact. [God.
De'i gra'ti a.—By the grace of
De ju're.—By right or law.
De no'vo.—Anew.

De sid er a'tum.—A thing desired.
Dic'tum.—A saying; a decision.
Dum viv'i mus vi va'mus.—While we live, let us live.
Ennui (*ong nwe'*).—Weariness.
E plu'ri bus u'num.—One formed of many; Motto of the U. S.
Er'go.—Therefore.
Et cet'e ra.—And so forth.
Ex cel si or.—More lofty.
Ex'e unt.—They go out.
Ex'it—He goes out; death.
Ex of fi'ci o.—By virtue of office.
Ex par'te.—On one side.
Ex post fac to.—After the deed is done. [itation.
Ex tem'po re.—Without premed-
Fac sim'i le.—A close imitation.
Fi nä'le.—The concluding piece in music; the close.
Fi'nis.—The end. [Father.
Glo'ri a Pa tri.—Glory be to the
Gra'tis.—For nothing; free.
Ha'be as cor'pus.—You may have
Hic ja'cet.—Here lies. [the body
Hors de combat (*or de cong bä'*) —Disabled; out of condition to fight. [the moment.
Im promp'tu.—On the spur of
Im pri'mis.—In the first place.
In cog'ni to.—Unknown.
In sta'tu quo.—In the former
In to to.—In the whole. [state.
In tran'si tu.—On the passage.
Ip'se dix'it.—He himself said it.
Ip'so fac'to.—In the fact itself.
Lap'sus lin guæ.—A slip of the tongue.
Laus De'o.—Praise God.
Lit er a'tim.—Letter for letter.
Mag'na Char'ta.—The great charter.
Ma'la fi de.—In bad faith.
Max'i mum.—The greatest.
Me lee (*ma la'*).—A conflict; a fight. [death.
Me men'to mo'ri.—Be mindful of
Min'i mum.—The smallest. [tell.
Mi rab'i le dic'tu.—Wonderful to
Mo'dus op er an'di.—Mode of operation. [little.
Mul'tum in par'vo.—Much in
Ne plus ul'tra.—The utmost extent. [willing.
No'lens vo'lens.—Unwilling or
Non com'pos men'tis.—Not of a sound mind.
O'ra pro no'bis.—Pray for us.
O're ro tun'do.—With round, full voice.
O tem'po ra! O mo'res!—O the times! O the manners!
Pa'ter nos'ter.—Our Father; the Lord's Prayer.
Per an'num.—By the year.
Per cen'tum.—By the hundred
Per di'em.—By the day.
Post mor'tem.—After death.
Pri'ma fa'ci e.—On the first view.
Pro bo'no pub'li co.—For the public good.
Pro et con.—For and against.
Pro ra'ta.—In proportion.
Pro tem'po re.—For the time.
Ren'o va te an'i mos.—Renew your courage. [Holies.
Sanc'tum sanc to'rum.—Holy of
Se cun'dum ar'tem.—According to art.
Sic sem'per ty ran'nis.—So may it ever be with tyrants.
Si'ne di'e.—Without day specified.
Si'ne qua non.—That which is indispensable. [fore.
Sta'tus quo—Same state as be-
Suav'i ter in mo'do.—Gentle in manners. [good.
Sum'mum bo'num.—The chief
Tem'pus fu'git.—Time flies.
Ter'ra fir'ma.—Solid earth.
Ul ti ma'tum.—The last or only condition.
U'na vo'ce.—With one voice.
Ul'tra.—Beyond; excessive.
Va'de me'cum.—Go with me.
Vi'ni, vi di, vi ci.—I came, I saw, I conquered.
Ver'sus.—Against.
Vi'ce ver'sa.—The terms being exchanged. [voice.
Vi'va vo'ce.—With the living
Vox pop'u li vox De'i.—The voice of the people is the voice of God.

SECTION XXIV.

CAPITAL LETTERS.

1. The first word of every sentence should begin with a capital; as, *Wisdom is better than rubies.*

2. The first word of every line of poetry should begin with a capital; as,

> "Farewell my friends! farewell my foes!
> My peace with these, my love to those."—BURNS.

3. I and O, when used as words, should be capitals; as, *I said I will be wise. O ye simple, understand wisdom.*

4. Every name of the Deity should begin with a capital; as, *God, Jehovah, the Almighty.*

5. Every proper name should begin with a capital; as, *Solomon, London.*

6. Titles of office and honor should begin with capitals; as, *Chief Justice Hale, Louis the Bold.*

7. The chief words in the titles of books should begin with capitals; as, *Pope's Essay on Man.*

8. Names of things persônified, should begin with capitals; as,

> "When Music, heavenly maid, was young."—COLLINS.

9. Words derived from proper names commonly begin with capitals; as, *American, Newtonian.*

10. Any word denoting a thing of special importance, may begin with a capital; as, *He supported the Reform Bill.*

PAUSES AND OTHER MARKS USED IN WRITING.

The Comma (,) denotes the shortest pause; the Semicolon (;) a pause double that of the comma; the Colon (:) a pause double that of the semicolon; and the Period (.) a pause double that of the colon.

The Interrogation point (?) denotes that a question is asked; as, *What is truth?*

The Exclamation point (!) denotes some strong or sudden emotion of the mind; as, *O death! where is thy sting!*

The Dash (—) denotes a sudden pause or change of subject.

The Parenthesis [( )] is used to include an explanatory sentence.

The Brackets ([ ]) are used to include words that serve to explain the preceding word or sentence ; as, *Newton* [*the Philosopher*], *was a great Astronomer.*

The Quotation (" ") is used to include a passage that is taken from some other author ; as, "*Know thyself.*"

The Apostrophe (') denotes the possessive case ; as, *John's hat ;* or the omission of one or more letters of a word ; as, *us'd* for *used.*

The Ellipsis (——) denotes that some letters in a word are omitted ; as *L——d* for *Lord.*

The Hyphen (-) is used to connect compound words ; as, *land-mark ;* also, to mark the division of a word.

The Caret (‸) is used to show that something has been
r *is*
omitted through mistake ; thus, *Chales ; Virtue amiable.*
^ ^

The Section (§) is used to divide a book or chapter into parts.

The Paragraph (¶) denotes the beginning of a new subject.

The Index or hand (☞) points out a paragraph, which is to be particularly observed.

The Asterisk (*), the Obelisk (†), the Double Dagger (‡), the Parallel (‖), and sometimes letters and figures, are used to refer the reader to notes in the margin, or at the bottom of the page.

The Brace (⏟) is used to connect several words with one common term.

The Diæresis (¨) is placed over the latter of two vowels, to show that they belong to two distinct syllables ; thus, *orthoëpy.*

www.ingramcontent.com/pod-product-compliance
Lightning Source LLC
LaVergne TN
LVHW011235110826
845150LV00006B/1642

* 9 7 8 1 4 2 5 5 1 3 8 4 9 *